THOMAS JEFFERSON

THOMAS JEFFERSON

Roger Bruns

Director of Publications
National Historical Publications and Records Commission
Washington, D.C.

1986
CHELSEA HOUSE PUBLISHERS

NEW YORK
NEW HAVEN   **PHILADELPHIA**

SENIOR EDITOR: William P. Hansen
ASSOCIATE EDITORS: John Haney
                   Richard Mandell
                   Marian W. Taylor
EDITORIAL COORDINATOR: Karyn Gullen Browne
EDITORIAL STAFF: Pierre Hauser
                  Perry Scott King
                  John Selfridge
                  Bert Yaeger
ART DIRECTOR: Susan Lusk
LAYOUT: Irene Friedman
ART ASSISTANTS: Ghila Krajzman
                 Carol McDougall
                 Tenaz Mehta
PICTURE RESEARCH: Mary Giunta
                   Julie Nichols
COVER: Frank Steiner

First Printing

Library of Congress Cataloging in Publication Data

Bruns, Roger. THOMAS JEFFERSON

(World Leaders Past & Present)
Bibliography: p.
Includes index
    1. Jefferson, Thomas, 1743–1826. 2. Presidents—
United States—Biography. [1. Jefferson, Thomas,
1743–1826. 2. Presidents] I. Title. II. Series.
E332.B918 1986   973.4′6′0924 [B] [92] 85—19056

ISBN 0-87754-583-9

Chelsea House Publishers
Harold Steinberg, Chairman & Publisher
Susan Lusk, Vice President
A Division of Chelsea House Educational Communications, Inc.

Chelsea House Publishers
133 Christopher Street
New York, N.Y. 10014

Photos courtesy of The Bettmann Archive, Library of Congress, National
Archives of France, National Archives and Records Administration, The
National Portrait Gallery, New York Public Library, The Second Bank of the
United States Portrait Gallery, Thomas Jefferson Memorial Foundation,
and the Virginia Museum

Contents

CHELSEA HOUSE PUBLISHERS

WORLD LEADERS PAST & PRESENT

ADENAUER	FRANCO	MAO
ALEXANDER THE GREAT	FREDERICK THE GREAT	MARY, QUEEN OF SCOTS
MARK ANTONY	INDIRA GANDHI	GOLDA MEIR
KING ARTHUR	GANDHI	METTERNICH
KEMAL ATATÜRK	GARIBALDI	MUSSOLINI
CLEMENT ATTLEE	GENGHIS KHAN	NAPOLEON
BEGIN	GLADSTONE	NASSER
BEN GURION	HAMMARSKJÖLD	NEHRU
BISMARCK	HENRY VIII	NERO
LEON BLUM	HENRY OF NAVARRE	NICHOLAS II
BOLÍVAR	HINDENBURG	NIXON
CESARE BORGIA	HITLER	NKRUMAH
BRANDT	HO CHI MINH	PERICLES
BREZHNEV	KING HUSSEIN	PERÓN
CAESAR	IVAN THE TERRIBLE	QADDAFI
CALVIN	ANDREW JACKSON	ROBESPIERRE
CASTRO	JEFFERSON	ELEANOR ROOSEVELT
CATHERINE THE GREAT	JOAN OF ARC	FDR
CHARLEMAGNE	POPE JOHN XXIII	THEODORE ROOSEVELT
CHIANG KAI-SHEK	LYNDON JOHNSON	SADAT
CHOU EN-LAI	BENITO JUÁREZ	SUN YAT-SEN
CHURCHILL	JFK	STALIN
CLEMENCEAU	KENYATTA	TAMERLAINE
CLEOPATRA	KHOMEINI	THATCHER
CORTEZ	KHRUSHCHEV	TITO
CROMWELL	MARTIN LUTHER KING	TROTSKY
DANTON	KISSINGER	TRUDEAU
DE GAULLE	LENIN	TRUMAN
DE VALERA	LINCOLN	QUEEN VICTORIA
DISRAELI	LLOYD GEORGE	WASHINGTON
EISENHOWER	LOUIS XIV	CHAIM WEIZMANN
ELEANOR OF AQUITAINE	LUTHER	WOODROW WILSON
QUEEN ELIZABETH I	JUDAS MACCABEUS	XERXES
FERDINAND AND ISABELLA		

Further titles in preparation

ON LEADERSHIP
Arthur M. Schlesinger, jr.

LEADERSHIP, it may be said, is really what makes the world go round. Love no doubt smooths the passage; but love is a private transaction between consenting adults. Leadership is a public transaction with history. The idea of leadership affirms the capacity of individuals to move, inspire and mobilize masses of people so that they act together in pursuit of an end. Sometimes leadership serves good purposes, sometimes bad; but whether the end is benign or evil, great leaders are those men and women who leave their personal stamp on history.

Now, the very concept of leadership implies the proposition that individuals can make a difference. This proposition has never been universally accepted. From classical times to the present day, eminent thinkers have regarded individuals as no more than the agents and pawns of larger forces, whether the gods and goddesses of the ancient world or, in the modern era, race, class, nation, the dialectic, the will of the people, the spirit of the times, history itself. Against such forces, the individual dwindles into insignificance.

So contends the thesis of historical determinism. Tolstoy's great novel *War and Peace* offers a famous statement of the case. Why, Tolstoy asked, did millions of men in the Napoleonic wars, denying their human feelings and their common sense, move back and forth across Europe slaughtering their fellows? "The war," Tolstoy answered, "was bound to happen simply because it was bound to happen." All prior history predetermined it. As for leaders, they, Tolstoy said, "are but the labels that serve to give a name to an end and, like labels, they have the least possible connection with the event." The greater the leader, "the more conspicuous the inevitability and the predestination of every act he commits." The leader, said Tolstoy, is "the slave of history."

Determinism takes many forms. Marxism is the determinism of class, Nazism the determinism of race. But the idea of men and women as the slaves of history runs athwart the deepest human instincts. Rigid determinism abolishes the idea of human freedom—the assumption of free choice that underlies every move we make, every word we speak, every thought we think. It abolishes the idea of human responsibility, since it is manifestly unfair to reward or punish people for actions that are by definition beyond their control. No one can live consistently by any deterministic creed. The Marxist states prove this themselves by their extreme susceptibility to the cult of leadership.

More than that, history refutes the idea that individuals make no difference. In December 1931 a British politician crossing Park Avenue in New York City between 76th and 77th Streets around ten-thirty at night looked in the wrong direction and was knocked down by an automobile—a moment, he later recalled, of a man aghast, a world aglare: "I do not understand why I was not broken like an eggshell or squashed like a gooseberry." Fourteen months later an American politician, sitting in an open car in Miami, Florida, was fired on by an assassin; the man beside him was hit. Those who believe that individuals make no difference to history might well ponder whether the next two decades would have been the same had Mario Contasini's car killed Winston Churchill in 1931 and Giuseppe Zangara's bullet killed Franklin Roosevelt in 1933. Suppose, in addition, that Adolf Hitler had been killed in the street fighting during the Munich *Putsch* of 1923 and that Lenin had died of typhus during the First World War. What would the 20th century be like now?

For better or for worse, individuals do make a difference. "The notion that a people can run itself and its affairs anonymously," wrote the philosopher William James, "is now well known to be the silliest of absurdities. Mankind does nothing save through initiatives on the part of inventors, great or small, and imitation by the rest of us—these are the sole factors in human progress. Individuals of genius show the way, and set the patterns, which common people then adopt and follow."

Leadership, James suggests, means leadership in thought as well as in action. In the long run, leaders in thought may well make the greater difference to the world. But, as Woodrow Wilson once said, "Those only are leaders of men, in the general eye, who lead in action. . . . It is at their hands that new thought gets its translation into the crude language of deeds." Leaders in thought often invent in solitude and obscurity, leaving to later generations the tasks of imitation. Leaders in action—the leaders portrayed in this series— have to be effective in their own time.

And they cannot be effective by themselves. They must act in response to the rhythms of their age. Their genius must be adapted, in a phrase of William James's, "to the receptivities of the moment." Leaders are useless without followers. "There goes the mob," said the French politician hearing a clamor in the streets. "I am their leader. I must follow them." Great leaders turn the inchoate emotions of the mob to purposes of their own. They seize on the opportunities of their time, the hopes, fears, frustrations, crises, potentialities.

They succeed when events have prepared the way for them, when the community is waiting to be aroused, when they can provide the clarifying and organizing ideas. Leadership ignites the circuit between the individual and the mass and thereby alters history.

It may alter history for better or for worse. Leaders have been responsible for the most extravagant follies and most monstrous crimes that have beset suffering humanity. They have also been vital in such gains as humanity has made in individual freedom, religious and racial tolerance, social justice and respect for human rights.

There is no sure way to tell in advance who is going to lead for good and who for evil. But a glance at the gallery of men and women in *World Leaders—Past and Present* suggests some useful tests.

One test is this: do leaders lead by force or by persuasion? By command or by consent? Through most of history leadership was exercised by the divine right of authority. The duty of followers was to defer and to obey. "Theirs not to reason why,/ Theirs but to do and die." On occasion, as with the so-called "enlightened despots" of the 18th century in Europe, absolutist leadership was animated by humane purposes. More often, absolutism nourished the passion for domination, land, gold and conquest and resulted in tyranny.

The great revolution of modern times has been the revolution of equality. The idea that all people should be equal in their legal condition has undermined the old structures of authority, hierarchy and deference. The revolution of equality has had two contrary effects on the nature of leadership. For equality, as Alexis de Tocqueville pointed out in his great study *Democracy in America*, might mean equality in servitude as well as equality in freedom.

"I know of only two methods of establishing equality in the political world," Tocqueville wrote. "Rights must be given to every citizen, or none at all to anyone . . . save one, who is the master of all." There was no middle ground "between the sovereignty of all and the absolute power of one man." In his astonishing prediction of 20th-century totalitarian dictatorship, Tocqueville explained how the revolution of equality could lead to the "*Führerprinzip*" and more terrible absolutism than the world had ever known.

But when rights are given to every citizen and the sovereignty of all is established, the problem of leadership takes a new form, becomes more exacting than ever before. It is easy to issue commands and enforce them by the rope and the stake, the concentration camp and the *gulag*. It is much harder to use argument and achievement to overcome opposition and win consent. The Founding Fathers of the United States understood the difficulty. They believed that history had given them the opportunity to decide, as

Alexander Hamilton wrote in the first Federalist Paper, whether men are indeed capable of basing government on "reflection and choice, or whether they are forever destined to depend . . . on accident and force."

Government by reflection and choice called for a new style of leadership and a new quality of followership. It required leaders to be responsive to popular concerns, and it required followers to be active and informed participants in the process. Democracy does not eliminate emotion from politics; sometimes it fosters demagoguery; but it is confident that, as the greatest of democratic leaders put it, you cannot fool all of the people all of the time. It measures leadership by results and retires those who overreach or falter or fail.

It is true that in the long run despots are measured by results too. But they can postpone the day of judgment, sometimes indefinitely, and in the meantime they can do infinite harm. It is also true that democracy is no guarantee of virtue and intelligence in government, for the voice of the people is not necessarily the voice of God. But democracy, by assuring the rights of opposition, offers built-in resistance to the evils inherent in absolutism. As the theologian Reinhold Niebuhr summed it up, "Man's capacity for justice makes democracy possible, but man's inclination to injustice makes democracy necessary."

A second test for leadership is the end for which power is sought. When leaders have as their goal the supremacy of a master race or the promotion of totalitarian revolution or the acquisition and exploitation of colonies or the protection of greed and privilege or the preservation of personal power, it is likely that their leadership will do little to advance the cause of humanity. When their goal is the abolition of slavery, the liberation of women, the enlargement of opportunity for the poor and powerless, the extension of equal rights to racial minorities, the defense of the freedoms of expression and opposition, it is likely that their leadership will increase the sum of human liberty and welfare.

Leaders have done great harm to the world. They have also conferred great benefits. You will find both sorts in this series. Even "good" leaders must be regarded with a certain wariness. Leaders are not demigods; they put on their trousers one leg after another just like ordinary mortals. No leader is infallible, and every leader needs to be reminded of this at regular intervals. Irreverence irritates leaders but is their salvation. Unquestioning submission corrupts leaders and demeans followers. Making a cult of a leader is always a mistake. Fortunately hero worship generates its own antidote. "Every hero," said Emerson, "becomes a bore at last."

The signal benefit the great leaders confer is to embolden the rest of us to live according to our own best selves, to be active, insistent, and resolute in affirming our own sense of things. For great leaders attest to the reality of human freedom against the supposed inevitabilities of history. And they attest to the wisdom and power that may lie within the most unlikely of us, which is why Abraham Lincoln remains the supreme example of great leadership. A great leader, said Emerson, exhibits new possibilities to all humanity. "We feed on genius. . . . Great men exist that there may be greater men."

Great leaders, in short, justify themselves by emancipating and empowering their followers. So humanity struggles to master its destiny, remembering with Alexis de Tocqueville: "It is true that around every man a fatal circle is traced beyond which he cannot pass; but within the wide verge of that circle he is powerful and free; as it is with man, so with communities."

—*New York*

1
The Declaration

Philadelphia, June 1776. A young Virginia delegate to the Continental Congress sits alone at a portable mahogany writing desk on the second floor of a brick house on Chestnut Street. Given the awesome task of drafting a document justifying the American Revolution, he pens the phrases soon to have such profound meaning to his fellow colonists. He works and reworks the sentences, trying for just the right images, the appropriate tone. The document gradually takes form. "We hold these truths to be self evident," writes Thomas Jefferson, "that all men are created equal, that they are endowed by their creator with certain inalienable rights; that among these are life, liberty, and the pursuit of happiness."

The words do not come easily. A man who sees Jefferson's manuscript observes that it is "scratched like a schoolboy's exercise." But the author continues to draft the mighty, thunderous phrases which will become so familiar to later generations. He writes that governments derive "their powers from the consent of the governed" and that any government that takes away those rights should be altered or abolished. He charges the British king, George III, with having conducted a reign of such tyranny that his American subjects have no choice

King George III (1738–1820), was, according to British law, the owner and absolute monarch of the American colonies. He regarded Thomas Jefferson's opinion—that a just government could rule only with the consent of the governed—as highly treasonous.

Thomas Jefferson (1743–1826) represents Virginia and Benjamin Franklin (1706–1790) Pennsylvania, as the Declaration of Independence is signed in Philadelphia on July 19, 1776. Written by Jefferson and edited by Franklin, John Adams (1735–1826), and Jefferson himself, the document was adopted by Congress on July 4.

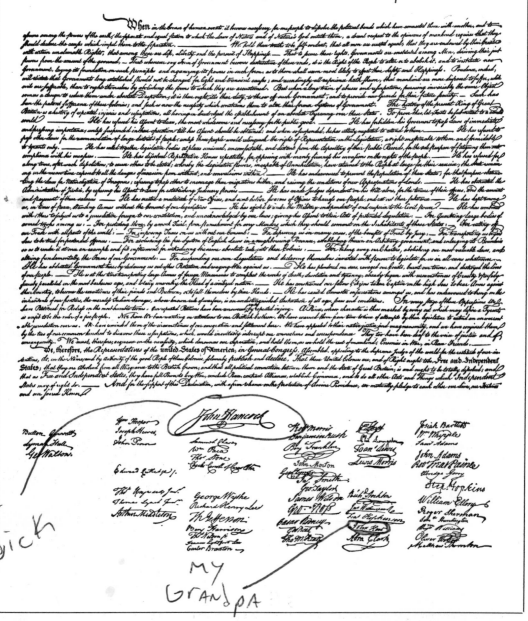

IN CONGRESS, JULY 4, 1776.

The unanimous Declaration of the thirteen united States of America.

The first copies of the Declaration of Independence contained none of the signatures seen here. Because the British declared that the act of signing the Declaration was high treason, punishable by death, the names of the signatories were kept secret for nearly a year.

but to revolt. He denies all allegiance to the king and declares the "colonies to be free and independent states." He concludes: "And for the support of this declaration we mutually pledge to each other our lives, our fortunes, and our sacred honor." This last was indeed a haunting pledge. During the coming war, some of Jefferson's fellow revolutionaries would lose their lives; many would lose their fortunes.

Jefferson completed the document in 17 days. In it was embodied the revolutionary spirit, growing national pride, and ideology of human equality that the colonial leaders had so forcefully expressed during the escalating conflict with the English crown. It was biting in attack but lofty in purpose. The Declaration of Independence would become the creed for a new nation.

At a dinner in 1962 honoring a considerable number of Nobel Prize winners, President John F. Kennedy called his assembled guests "the most extraordinary collection of talents . . . that has ever gathered together at the White House, with the possible exception of when Thomas Jefferson dined alone." Who was this man Jefferson to draw such praise? John Kennedy, himself a man of much learning and perception, was also a student of history. He knew well the story of Jefferson, knew of the legacy of the man whose ideas and deeds were so central to the early history of the country. Statesman, diplomat, author, scientist, architect, politi-

A colonial schoolmaster listens to a student read a lesson from his slate. There were few public schools in the Virginia of Jefferson's day; families who could afford to educate their children usually sent them to private classes taught by local members of the clergy.

cian, political theorist, inventor—Jefferson was all of these. He was, in an age of many great men, one of the most extraordinary.

He was born on April 13, 1743, the third child of Peter and Jane Jefferson. The site of the birth was Shadwell, a plantation in Virginia, on the banks of the Rivanna River in what is now Albemarle County. His father was a prominent, self-made landholder, surveyor, and mapmaker; his mother was the eldest daughter of Scottish-born Isham Randolph, a wealthy James River planter. A man of little formal schooling but of varied interests, a man who especially delighted in exploring the Virginia wilderness, Peter Jefferson had an active, inquiring mind, a quality his son Thomas always displayed in abundance. Peter Jefferson wanted his son to have the kind of education he himself lacked. Thus, in his early years, young Thomas was taught by private tutors, and much of his youth was spent away from home as a boarding student.

Thomas was only 14 years old when his father died. One of Peter Jefferson's last wishes was that his boy receive a classical education. As the family was now very influential in the county and had sizable holdings in rich tobacco lands and slaves, Peter Jefferson's intentions for his oldest son were easily realized.

Thomas soon joined the Reverend James Maury, an Anglican pastor and one of the colony's better-educated men, at his Fredericksville parish and school. It was here, in a log schoolhouse about a dozen miles from his birthplace at the Shadwell plantation, that Thomas became acquainted with the vast world of books and learning, a world into which he would continue to plunge all his life.

Greek, Latin, the English classics, history—the young Jefferson began to study them all eagerly. Maury, with his large library, provided the setting for what Jefferson later remembered as some of the happiest days of his life. Mixed in with the intellectual excitement were the days of chasing deer, fox, and wild turkey in the mountains, of hiking, and of horseback riding. Maury took his students on treks through the Blue Ridge Mountains in search

Jefferson enjoyed walking, particularly in the beautiful, stream-crossed Blue Ridge Mountains. He often recommended walking as the best form of exercise, and advised walkers to carry a gun, which, he said, "gives boldness, enterprise, and independence to the mind."

of fossils. In addition to all this, Thomas learned to dance and to play the violin.

In January 1760, at age 16, Jefferson wrote a letter to a friend expressing a desire to widen his circle of acquaintances, to see more of the world, and to further his education beyond the hills of Albemarle County. Of the thousands of letters that Jefferson penned in his lifetime, it is the oldest one that survives today. "As long as I stay at the Mountains," he wrote, "the Loss of one fourth of my Time is inevitable, by Company's coming here and detaining me from School." These are fairly solemn words from a 16-year-old, this concern that too many visitors at home might rob him of study time. But this quest for knowledge, this passion for books and learning, was typical of Jefferson throughout his long life.

In the spring of 1760 Jefferson traveled to Williamsburg, the capital of Virginia, to enroll in the College of William and Mary. For the 17-year-old from the Albemarle hills, the Williamsburg culture held fascinations never before experienced. There were the buildings such as the porticoed Capitol and the magnificent governor's mansion, there were the fashionable stores, the well-to-do families riding in expensive coaches, the politicians and lawyers sporting colorful knee breeches and coats, accompanied by their ladies showing off imported dresses as they strolled along Duke of Gloucester Street. There were tradesmen, shopkeepers, craftsmen, and slaves also walking the bustling city streets. There were the acting companies to see and balls to dance at. There were the taverns, especially the Raleigh, where diners ate venison, stew, and Welsh rarebit and drank punch, brandy, rum, and French wines.

Jefferson was less impressed, however, with the college itself. The building, recently remodeled after a fire, was hardly more than a pile of bricks covered with a roof. And the students were generally less advanced in their studies than the young gentleman of Shadwell. But it was here that Jefferson met Doctor William Small, a professor of mathematics and philosophy who quickly took Jefferson

Virginians socialize before church. Because regular churchgoing was expected of Williamsburg residents, Jefferson attended services when he was a college student, but he had little interest—then or later—in formal religion. "I not only write nothing on religion," he said in 1815, "but rarely permit myself to speak of it."

George Washington (1732–1799) was, like his successor Jefferson, a music-lover. The nation's first president was extremely fond of dancing and concerts; some historians say he also played the flute. Here, his stepdaughter, Nellie Custis, accompanies him as his wife, Martha Custis Washington (1732–1802), listens.

He always loved the red hills of Albemarle more than the streets of any city. He kept returning to this native region until finally he came home for good, and in his heart of hearts he was always there.

—DUMAS MALONE
American historian

under his wing. Through Small he was introduced to George Wythe, a prominent lawyer and professor who would become his teacher, and Lieutenant-Governor Francis Fauquier, an economist and student of physics and natural sciences, a man of cultivated tastes and manners. Seated at tavern tables sipping glasses of port, these three men opened up to the young Jefferson new and exciting horizons of knowledge—art, navigation, philosophy, political theory, natural history, and law. He took it all in, his gifted, probing mind challenged and invigorated.

Jefferson now had the impressive physical stature that would always mark him in a crowd—the imposing height, especially for that day, of 6 feet, 3 inches; the striking, tousled red hair; and the strong, ruddy face. Although a diligent, serious student who was often alone with his books, Jefferson acquired several close friends at the school, including John Tyler, whose son would become the tenth president of the United States. Both men loved to play the violin and they belonged to a small musical group. The two were sometimes interrupted in mid-study late at night by their fellow roommate, Frank Willis, an unrestrained practical joker. The future author of the Declaration of Independence often had his study table overturned and books carried off by young Willis.

The talented youth from Shadwell, possessed of land and money and learning, could look forward with near certainty to success and a full, rich life. But in what field? In 1762 Jefferson decided to become an apprentice to George Wythe as a student in the law, not a surprising choice given Jefferson's close friendship with, and enormous respect for, the esteemed Williamsburg lawyer. Lawyers in the colony were making great reputations and exerting much influence. Patrick Henry was one. Jefferson had heard the stirring speeches of the fiery orator and wrote later, "I have frequently shut my eyes while he spoke and where he got that torrent of language is unconceivable."

For five years Jefferson, like most young men studying for the law in colonial Virginia, ran errands for his employer, accompanied him to court, attended various meetings and functions in Williamsburg, met other influential lawyers, and kept voluminous notes. He learned by watching and doing. There were no required courses, no set books that all students were obliged to read. In fact, during his apprenticeship Jefferson was more often at Shadwell than in Williamsburg, helping to care for the family farm. But his wide reading continued—philosophy, literature, and such writings on the law as Lord Kames's "Historical Law Tracts." He began to acquire a large personal library. Jefferson was now achieving a deep understanding of the law and the legal structure on which colonial Vir-

A horseback rider of Jefferson's day protects himself from rain and sun with a wide-brimmed planter's hat. Jefferson was a superb horseman, but he sometimes worried that riding was a lazy man's form of travel. "A horse," he complained, "gives but a kind of half-exercise."

The master of Monticello oversees the work of a slave. Jefferson was never quite content away from his hilltop home. From Paris, he wrote a friend: "I am savage enough to prefer the woods, the wilds, and the independence of Monticello to all the brilliant pleasures of this gay capital."

Mr. Jefferson is quite tall, six feet, one or two inches, face streaked and speckled with red, light grey eyes, white hair, dressed in shoes of very soft leather, grey worsted stockings, corduroy small clothes, blue waistcoat and overcoat of stiff thick cloth badly manufactured. His figure bony, long and with broad shoulders, a true Virginian.
—FRANCIS CALLEY GRAY
American writer and
contemporary of Jefferson

ginia rested, as well as an appreciation of the sciences, the arts, and other areas of thought so often discussed and debated by his extraordinary teachers—Wythe, Small, and the others. The young law apprentice was rapidly becoming a learned man.

It was said that Thomas Jefferson sometimes spent 14 hours a day at his studies. But he was in no way a recluse or dull bookworm. Although reserved and somewhat shy, he loved good times and enjoyed warm companionship. He charged into his leisure with the same kind of enthusiasm he devoted to his studies. He was a good horseman and dancer. He caught the eye of many young women and returned their glances with equal interest.

Very early in 1762 he fell in love with a 16-year-old named Rebecca Burwell, whom he seriously considered marrying. One night at a gala ball in the Apollo Room of Raleigh's Tavern, he muttered of his affections in "a few broken sentences . . . in great disorder, and interrupted with pauses of uncommon length." He later managed to make a fumbling speech to her about his possible marital intentions. The erudite student, so proficient with pen, was hopelessly tongue-tied in front of Rebecca Burwell. The young lady decided to marry someone else. To make matters even more humiliating, the victorious beau, unaware that Jefferson too had been pursuing Rebecca, asked him to be the best man at the wedding.

Jefferson's romantic fiasco temporarily soured

his opinion of women. He wrote to a friend after Rebecca's engagement, "Well the Lord bless her, I say! . . . Many and great are the comforts of a single state." He was now determined never to be so swept away by infatuation, never to allow the fascination of womankind to interfere with his drive for learning and a career. Marriage? "When I am old and weary of the world."

In 1767, at the age of 24, Jefferson was admitted to the bar of the General Court of Virginia. For the next seven years he would take on hundreds of cases, most of which involved disputes over land and property rights. Many were tried in the county courts and therefore required long horseback rides across Virginia. Accompanied by a slave named Jupiter, Jefferson made the rounds and established a thriving practice. He gained great understanding of Virginian society and politics, and made friendships that would prove valuable in the coming years. He was not a good orator—nothing approaching a Patrick Henry—but he was extraordinarily thorough, and conducted painstaking research in preparation for most cases.

In addition to his legal duties, Jefferson remained responsible for the Shadwell plantation. There were fences and roads and bridges to be built, trees and vegetables to be planted, horses to be bought and sold, tobacco to be marketed, slaves to be managed. With the encouragement and advice of Philip Mazzei, a neighbor and Italian immigrant, Jefferson even began to experiment with the cultivation of European vegetables and fruits. Truly, Jefferson's interests were unbounded. He studied many new areas of learning and recorded facts in journals, books about the farm, account books, and garden books. He recorded almost everything known to him. His mind was ordered, precise, and logical.

While Jefferson began law practice and tended to affairs at Shadwell, the political climate in America was becoming increasingly tumultuous as the first echoes of colonial protest began to sound against British rule. Jefferson's colony of Virginia, the largest and most populous in America, would soon be at the center of the turmoil.

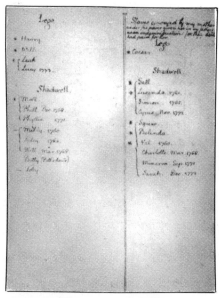

A page from one of Jefferson's meticulously kept farm books shows the names and birth years of slaves who worked at Lego and Shadwell, farms adjoining Monticello.

2
Seeds of Revolution

Whenever any form of government becomes destructive, it is the right of the people to alter or to abolish it.
—THOMAS JEFFERSON
quoted from the
Declaration of Independence

Thomas Jefferson had seen the growing discontent with England felt by many of the colonists. They bitterly resented the Stamp Act, a law passed by the British Parliament in 1765, which required a tax stamp on almost every conceivable colonial document. Since the colonists had no representation in Parliament, they insisted that the measure constituted an imposition against which they had no means to appeal. The tax fell heavily on many of the most educated men in the colonies—lawyers, politicians, clergymen, and all others whose business generated documents. They were also, however, the men most capable of fighting back.

Jefferson was a member of the audience in the Virginia legislature on the day when a strident Patrick Henry, fiercely attacking British colonial policy, ended his speech with the famous and defiant words, "If this be treason, make the most of it." Jefferson was dazzled by Henry's flood of words and always credited him with setting in motion "the ball of revolution."

Why was Patrick Henry so furious over British policy? Where had all this discontent come from? It sprang in part from the earlier French and Indian War, which had pitted England against France

John Stuart (1713–1792), a Scottish noble and favorite of George III, served as Britain's prime minister from 1762 to 1763. A staunch believer in absolute monarchy, he voted against the repeal of the Stamp Act in 1766.

The Stamp Act inspired riots like this one in every colonial seaport. Calling themselves "the Sons of Liberty," groups of citizens attacked government officials, seizing and burning the stamp paper for which England demanded taxes. No one was killed, but the crown got the message and nullified the act four months after its imposition.

Israel Putnam (1718–1790), a major in the British Army, is rescued by a fellow officer during the French and Indian War in 1758. After the Battle of Lexington, Putnam enlisted in the Continental Army and was commissioned a major general. He fought the British at Bunker Hill, New York, and Philadelphia.

> *There is not in the British empire a man who more cordially loves a union with Great Britain than I do. But by the God that made me, I will cease to exist before I yield to a connection on such terms as the British Parliament proposes.*
> —THOMAS JEFFERSON
> writing in 1775

for control of North America. The war had ended in 1763 with the British victorious. Having expelled the French from most of North America, England had set out to establish more effective control over its possessions there. Part of that effort had been a move to force Americans to pay a larger share of the expenses of the British Empire, in effect to help pay for the war in America. The Stamp Act, however, a reasonable measure from the point of view of the Crown, was thoroughly obnoxious to many American leaders. Patrick Henry's speech, though the most passionate, was only one of many hostile messages fired at England by its American subjects.

In the face of strong resistance from colonial leaders the British government had backed down and repealed the Stamp Act. But the abatement of controversy was not to last. A year later the British Parliament once again asserted its authority. The Townshend Acts of 1767 provided for fresh taxes on tea, paper, ink, and glass. The new measures rekindled colonial anger, and the cries of protest became even more forceful.

Thomas Jefferson's stature in Virginia was rising just as the hostility between England and America was becoming more threatening. In December 1768 he was elected to the Virginia House of Burgesses, an unusual achievement for a man of only 26, a man who had never before held any public office in the colony. In this time of growing political struggles a seat in the House of Burgesses would be crucial and significant. Jefferson would now be at the center of colonial affairs.

In 1769, the House of Burgesses adopted resolutions that argued against the British Parliament's right to tax. The resolutions demanded that the people of Virginia, not members of Parliament sitting halfway around the world, should have the right to decide what taxes should be raised in Virginia, and for what purposes. Quickly retaliating, the colonial governor, who favored the British in the dispute, dissolved the House of Burgesses. Its angry officials soon reassembled in the Apollo Room of the Raleigh Tavern, the same room in which Thomas Jefferson had years before found so much difficulty expressing his affection for Rebecca Burwell. Here in the Raleigh, the Virginia burgesses entered into an agreement. They pledged not to buy goods taxed by Parliament. The agreement was designed to hurt British merchants and force Parliament to repeal the hated Townshend tax laws. The boycott was an open act of rebellion.

In the months following, similar agreements were drawn up in other colonies. The British once again bowed to the rising discontent, removing all the taxes except for that on tea. But the hostility did not slacken. As long as the tax on tea remained in effect, colonial dissatisfaction would continue. To the young, red-haired delegate from Albemarle County, the British policies seemed outrageous. He was now firmly pitted against British oppression, determined to fight hard against "colonial subservience" to England. The colonists, he believed, must stand up for their rights.

Further north, the increasing colonial anger had reached violent levels and brought tragic results. In 1770 several colonists in Boston provoked British soldiers on duty there into a riotous battle in which several citizens were killed and others wounded. The colonists, using the event for propaganda purposes, called it "The Boston Massacre."

In the face of what they saw as British tyranny, a

"Fire and be damned, we know you dare not!" Thus taunted, British sentries aimed their muskets at a Boston waterfront crowd on the chilly night of March 5, 1770. The ensuing "Boston Massacre" took the lives of three colonists, including Crispus Attucks, the first black to die in the struggle for liberty.

Jefferson's beautiful home at Monticello took shape from the many sketches he made before construction began. Sold after its owner's death, the estate was abandoned for a number of years. It was bought and restored by a foundation in 1923, and is now a national shrine open to the public.

number of colonial leaders formed committees of correspondence to provide easier communication between the various colonies in the growing conflict. In these early committees were the makings of a united front of the American colonies against the British, the beginnings of a widespread revolt. The fires of war lay ahead.

For now, however, Thomas Jefferson's private life had to deal with a fire of a different kind. In February 1770 the house at Shadwell burned to the ground. In the terrible blaze the young lawyer lost almost all of his papers and books. But the catastrophe motivated him to devote more energy to a project he had begun three years earlier—the building of a new home. Across the Rivanna River from Shadwell was what Jefferson called his "little mountain," or, in Italian, "Monticello." It was here, overlooking the rolling hills and rich, deep valleys, that Jefferson would build a magnificent estate. He had already begun to make drawings and to saw lumber and plant fruit trees on the hill. Building on such a height was unusual. To make transportation convenient, most Virginia plantations were situated along rivers. For Jefferson, though, architecture had become another passion and Monticello a challenge. He would design his own house, would place it on a hill, and serve as his own architect.

Ever since he had obtained a book on architecture from an old cabinetmaker, he had been enthralled with the subject and with plans for the Monticello project. For some 40 years, Jefferson would be absorbed in the construction, designing, and redesigning of the house. By November 1770 he was able to move into the South Pavilion, the first part of the estate to be completed. "I have here but one room," he wrote, "which, like the cobbler's, serves me for parlor, for kitchen and hall . . . for bed chamber and study too." It would not always be this way. The grandeur of the Monticello estate was now taking form. Within a decade it would be one of the most magnificent architectural achievements in America.

After his frustrated romance with Rebecca Burwell, Jefferson had praised the glories of the bachelor state. As for marriage, he had scoffed, he would wait till he was old. Martha Wayles Skelton changed his mind. This recently widowed 23-year-old was attractive and an heir to a large fortune. She had one child from her marriage, a boy named John. She was socially graceful, well read and educated, and a superb dancer who also played the harpsichord and spinet. She was also experienced in managing the affairs of a household—keeping accounts, supervising the slaves, tending to their illnesses, and hosting receptions. Under the charms of this remarkable woman, Jefferson's hesitation about marriage wilted.

On December 3, 1771, Jefferson filled out a formal application for a marriage license in the court of Charles City County, and on New Year's Day the two were married. Through a heavy snowstorm the

Spectators cheer the "Boston Tea Party," the celebrated raid staged by 150 colonists disguised as Indians. Boarding three British merchant ships, they emptied 342 chests of tea into the harbor's icy waters on the night of December 16, 1773. One of the "party" was said to be Paul Revere (1735–1818).

The colonists' political friends in Britain considered Jefferson's *Summary View of the Rights of British America* the best statement of the American position. After its London publication, the British government added Jefferson's name to its list of "dangerous subjects," which already included such "traitors" as John Adams, Samuel Adams (1722–1803), and Patrick Henry.

In a back room of Williamsburg's Raleigh Tavern, Thomas Jefferson (left) and Richard Henry Lee (1732–1794) draft a letter advocating the formation of a Continental Congress. Standing is Patrick Henry (1736–1799), the lawyer, patriot, and orator who later said, "Give me liberty, or give me death!"

A

SUMMARY VIEW

OF THE

R I G H T S

OF

BRITISH AMERICA.

SET FORTH IN SOME

RESOLUTIONS

INTENDED FOR THE

INSPECTION

OF THE PRESENT

DELEGATES

OF THE

PEOPLE OF VIRGINIA.

NOW IN

CONVENTION.

BY A NATIVE, AND MEMBER OF THE
HOUSE, OF BURGESSES.
by Thomas Jefferson

28-year-old Jefferson rode with his new bride to Monticello. The one room, he wrote, became his "Honeymoon Lodge." September brought the joy of their first child, a girl they named Martha. Frail and weak as an infant, she gradually gained the robust strength that so characterized her father. A second daughter, born a year and a half later, was not as fortunate as Martha. She died before the end of 1775. Of six children born to Thomas and Martha Jefferson only two survived infancy. In ad-

John Malcolm, a Boston customs officer, is tarred and feathered by an angry mob on January 24, 1774. The unfortunate official had made the mistake of trying to collect British taxes on imported merchandise.

dition, in May 1773 Jefferson's infant stepson also died. Jefferson's happiness on the mountain there was combined with much grief.

Thomas Jefferson was now one of the richest landowners of his county, one of the most successful lawyers in Virginia, and a member of the assembly. He was also happily married, busy with the building and managing of his estate, and absorbed in his reading. In other times he could have looked forward to the ideal life of the gentleman farmer and scholar. But these were not other times. Events were about to bring Thomas Jefferson to the front and center of a larger stage.

In December 1773 a group of men thinly disguised as Mohawk Indians gathered at the Boston harbor, boarded the ship *Dartmouth*, which carried tea for the British East India Company, and dumped the entire cargo into the water. The British government reacted swiftly and angrily by closing the port until the company received compensation for the tea lost at the so-called "Boston Tea Party." Parliament also severely limited the colonists' rights in Massachusetts. The Americans began to refer to the new measures laid down by Britain as "The Intolerable Acts."

When news of these measures reached the Virginia Assembly in June 1774, a small group of lawyers led by Patrick Henry and Richard Henry Lee decided to intensify their attacks on the Brit-

The regulation uniform for enlisted men in the Continental Army included a blue coat made in France. Supplies were short, however, and most soldiers—officers and enlisted men alike—wore ordinary clothes combined with whatever military gear they could find.

Patrick Henry's fiery oratory helped to advance the American Revolution. After the war, however, he became a staunch opponent of the proposed Constitution, asserting that it "squinted toward monarchy" by giving too much power to the president. Nevertheless, when the Constitution was ratified, he promised to support it.

ish by taking a determined stand in favor of the Massachusetts patriots. Meeting once again at the Raleigh Tavern, the Virginians proposed that the committees of correspondence in the various colonies appoint delegates to meet in a congress of all the colonies, a "Continental Congress." This would be a legislative body formed to take united measures against British oppression. An attack against any one colony, the Virginians asserted, should be considered an attack against all of the colonies.

Thomas Jefferson had reached the conclusion that the colonists must be subject to no laws except those passed by themselves, and that all the American colonies must be free from the control of the British Parliament. Many other American leaders at this time favored a more cautious approach, hoping to solve the current disputes while continuing to exist under English rule. Jefferson's ideas, compared to the views of these men, were radical indeed.

In 1774 Jefferson presented his views in one of the most significant documents published in this period—*A Summary View of the Rights of British America.* The document was written for the purpose of instructing the Virginia delegates who would attend the Continental Congress. A convention was held in Williamsburg in August 1774 to select those delegates, but it did not approve Jefferson's paper. It decided, instead, to approve a milder position on the questions of the colonists' rights within the British Empire. Even George Wythe, Jefferson's close friend, and George Washington, the influential planter from Mount Vernon, favored a more friendly approach toward Britain.

Although the convention did not accept Jefferson's proposals, some of his friends published it as a pamphlet in Williamsburg, and it was reprinted in Philadelphia and later in England. It made a national figure out of Thomas Jefferson and established him as one of the most influential writers of the time.

In the paper Jefferson claimed that the colonists in America were under no special obligation to remain controlled by the British Parliament, and that nature had given to all men the right to leave a country, to seek new places to live, to set up their own governments, and establish their own laws. When the first settlers had left England for America, Jefferson insisted, they had severed ties with the mother country and had regained full possession of their natural right to create a new society and government. England had no right to continue to exercise power over the colonists in America.

Jefferson did not advocate revolution against England in the *Summary View*. While renouncing all authority of Parliament, he did not claim complete independence from the British king—although kings, he declared, were the servants of the people, not their masters. But his words were leading directly toward the final break; he was at the edge.

Although some other American leaders were not yet ready for this kind of statement, Jefferson, in this forceful assertion of colonial liberty, had sounded a battle cry, had raised the flag under which patriots with views similar to his own could gather. The gentleman farmer and lawyer from Monticello was in the forefront of a growing colonial movement.

The Continental Congress assembled in Philadelphia in September 1774 under the presidency of Peyton Randolph, another influential leader from Virginia. It officially condemned most British tax

The Battle of Lexington. As British soldiers marched toward Concord, Massachusetts, on April 18, 1775, Paul Revere galloped ahead to warn the colonists. When the British reached Lexington the next day, the local militia was waiting for them on the village common. Shots were fired, and eight patriots soon lay dead on the green.

measures and formed the so-called Continental Association, joining the colonies in an agreement to attack Britain economically by refusing to import and buy British goods. Meanwhile, in Massachusetts companies of "minutemen" were secretly drilling and stocking arms and ammunition, preparing for armed clashes.

In March 1775 Jefferson attended a convention of Virginia representatives and heard Patrick Henry deliver the speech that above all others set the tone of the drive for independence. "Our chains are forged," he roared. "Their clanking may be heard on the plains of Boston! The war is inevitable—and let it come! . . . I know not what course others may take; but as for me, give me liberty, or give me death!"

Henry's words were soon followed by the rumble of war hundreds of miles to the north in Massachusetts. At Concord and Lexington, British soldiers fought with colonial militia. Many were killed and injured on both sides. Patrick Henry had called war "inevitable." He had been right.

As cries for war increased, many individuals were wrenched apart by conflicting loyalties and sympathies. After all, they were British subjects, with close attachments to British history, customs, and law. But they also now had loyalties to their own American colonies. As their links to British heritage and ways clashed with their growing feeling of identity in America, many colonists had to make painful decisions. Some stayed in America and

British troops, continuing their march from Lexington on April 19, are met and defeated by 500 armed colonists in Concord, Massachusetts. Ralph Waldo Emerson (1803–1882) immortalized the day in his poem about Concord, "where the embattled farmers stood, and fired the shot heard round the world."

Philadelphia, site of the second Continental Congress in 1775, was the largest and most prosperous city in North America. Many of its paved streets were lighted by whale-oil lamps, and it boasted fine public buildings, three libraries, three newspapers, a college, and the only hospital in the colonies.

joined the patriot cause; others returned to England. Some remained in America but maintained their British loyalties.

In the midst of this growing turmoil Thomas Jefferson was appointed a delegate to the Continental Congress in 1775. The most important colonial leaders in America would now meet and work with the young lawyer from Virginia, the author of the *Summary View.* Jefferson was only 33 years of age, one of the youngest members of the Continental Congress. But his impact on revolutionary America lay immediately ahead.

It was here in Philadelphia—here in this colonial center for art, science, education, and commerce, here on the bluffs overlooking the Schuykill and Delaware rivers, here on these cobblestone walks, in these ivy-covered courtyards, and austere Quaker meetinghouses—that the fortunes of the American colonies hung in the balance. How would all these representatives from different colonies with their separate interests and customs work together? Could the representatives of the various parts of the country forge a unified front? Was the protest and agitation a march toward disaster?

Jefferson soon made a favorable impression upon many in the Continental Congress. John Adams remembered the first few weeks after Jefferson's arrival: "Mr. Jefferson came into Congress in June

Enlighten the people generally, and tyranny and oppressions of body and mind will vanish like evil spirits at the dawn of day.
—THOMAS JEFFERSON

Samuel Adams, a well-educated Bostonian and master propagandist, was one of the principal organizers of the movement for independence. A true revolutionary whose motto was "Take a stand at the start," he believed that any concessions to Britain would result in the complete subjugation of the 13 American colonies.

1775, and brought with him a reputation for literature, science, and a happy talent of composition . . . though a silent member in Congress, he was so prompt, frank, explicit and decisive upon committees and in conversation . . . that he soon seized my heart."

It was a spirited, youthful, talented group of men who made up this Continental Congress. From all over colonial America they came: Benjamin Franklin of Pennsylvania, the oldest member, an almost legendary philosopher, diplomat, inventor, a man whom Jefferson greatly admired and respected; John and Samuel Adams of Massachusetts, cousins, both strong for challenging the British at every turn, for asserting American liberties as far as possible; John Dickinson of Pennsylvania, cautious, reluctant to push Parliament too far; John Jay of New York, extraordinarily learned, with a legalistic mind much like Jefferson's. All these men had earned substantial reputations in their own colonies; most were suspicious of the other members, guarded in manner but, at the same time, aware that cooperation and compromise were of vital importance.

Following the violence between colonists and British soldiers at Lexington and Concord, the members of Congress had voted to put the colonies in a state of defense, authorizing the formation of an army. Shortly after Jefferson arrived in Philadelphia, news of another battle, that at Bunker Hill in Massachusetts, reached the city. Amidst much growing war fever and public demonstrations in the marketplaces, Congress appointed George Washington, who had distinguished himself in the French and Indian War, to take command of the Continental army near Boston. Jefferson wrote home that the "war is now heartily entered into. . . ."

But even if war had already begun, most citizens in America assumed it was a war between Englishmen, that in all likelihood a permanent break would be avoided. As for Jefferson, he wrote that he would prefer to be under British rule than under that of any other nation. But rather than submit to the continued outrages of Parliament, he said, he would lend his support to sink Britain, sink the "whole island in the ocean."

The Congress was now engaged in the mass of activities related to carrying on a war—finding military officers, raising money, establishing military regulations, opening new sources of trade with foreign countries. Jefferson was soon appointed to a committee to draft a document explaining the reasons why the colonies felt it necessary to take up arms against England. Jefferson's paper, a strong, harsh attack against Parliament, was rejected by the committee as too belligerent. John Dickinson, a less radical delegate, modified the paper. But even with Dickinson's changes, the paper, entitled *Declaration of the Cause and Necessity for Taking Up Arms*, called Parliament's actions violent and tyrannical. The American colonists were "re-

Benjamin Franklin, like Jefferson, both signed and helped to write the Declaration of Independence. Renowned as a philosopher, statesman, inventor, and scientist, Franklin was also a wit: "Now we must all hang together," he said to his fellow signers of the Declaration, "or we shall all hang separately."

solved to die Freemen rather than to live Slaves." This was a momentous and shattering period in American history, a time of great deeds, deep soul-searching, great oratory, and bloody battles. And Thomas Jefferson was at the center of it.

The master of Monticello, however, longed for his family and the beloved hills and valleys of Virginia. He returned briefly to his home in August 1775, only to see his infant daughter, Jane Randolph, pass away soon after he arrived. Both his wife and mother were also in poor health.

When he went back to Philadelphia in September, Jefferson's anxieties over his family remained intense. He wrote home to his brother-in-law, "The suspense under which I am is too terrible to be endured. If anything has happened, for God's sake let me know it."

Three days after Christmas, while Congress continued its important deliberations, Jefferson, one of its most influential members, was once again on the road back to Monticello. When he arrived he found his wife ill but recovering. His mother, however, was failing rapidly and died a few months later. Jefferson remained at Monticello until May 1776, he and his family sustaining each other through their trials of illness and death.

Meanwhile, several events beyond the hills of Albemarle County brought the American colonies closer to an outright break with the British. In August 1775 King George III issued a proclamation declaring his American subjects to be "engaged in open and avowed rebellion" for the purpose of establishing an independent empire. A number of royal governors in the colonies abandoned all hope

The Battle of Bunker Hill (June 17, 1776) was a tactical victory for the British, but a strategic and moral triumph for the Americans, whose losses were vastly exceeded by the redcoats'. It was at Bunker Hill that Colonel William Prescott (1726–1795) uttered the famous war cry, "Don't fire till you see the whites of their eyes!"

Citizens of New York pull down a statue of George III after a public reading of the Declaration of Independence on July 9, 1776. Americans were not enthusiastic about war, but most of them supported it as the only alternative to what they considered "slavery."

of reaching a peaceful settlement and went home to England. They not only feared for their declining power but also for their lives. The British evacuated Boston under the threat of the colonists' growing military strength.

In January 1776 a pamphlet entitled *Common Sense* began to circulate among the colonists like a political whirlwind. It was written by a former corsetmaker who had recently arrived in America from England—Thomas Paine. A man of relative poverty who had wandered from job to job for most of his life, Paine had befriended Benjamin Franklin in England. With Franklin's encouragement, he came to Philadelphia in 1774 and for a time worked for the *Pennsylvania Magazine*. And now, in 1776, Paine published the essay which the prominent Philadelphia physician and political leader Benjamin Rush observed "burst from the press with an effect which has rarely been produced by type and paper in any age or country."

"These are the times that try men's souls," the essay began. "Government by Kings was introduced into the world by the Heathens." Monarchy, Paine sneered, was nonsense. Here, in stark, vicious prose, Paine made the case for American independence brashly and defiantly. Jefferson read the essay at Monticello. Although probably repelled by its tone, he agreed with most of its sentiments. So did many

All honor to Jefferson—to the man who, in the concrete pressure of a struggle for national independence by a single people, had the coolness, forecast, and capacity to introduce into a merely revolutionary document an abstract truth, applicable to all men and all times, and so embalm it there that today and in all coming days it shall be a rebuke and a stumbling block to the very harbingers of reappearing tyranny and oppression.
—ABRAHAM LINCOLN
president of the United States
(1861–65)

Jefferson spent 18 days in this Philadelphia house composing the first draft of the Declaration of Independence. When he was asked to write it, Jefferson protested that a senior committee member, such as John Adams, would be a better choice. Adams disagreed. "You write," he told the younger man, "ten times better than I do."

Thomas Paine (1737—1809) was regarded as a hero after he published *Common Sense*, a 47-page pamphlet that influenced history by strongly advocating immediate independence. He became the object of public scorn, however, when he criticized religion in his 1794 book, *The Age of Reason*, and died penniless and obscure.

others. Even cautious George Wythe, Jefferson's law teacher, was now moved to remark, "Why should we be so fond of calling ourselves dutiful subjects?"

In May 1776 Jefferson once again left his family and home for Philadelphia, aware that truly significant events lay immediately ahead. Should the colonial leaders decide to declare independence from Britain, all of their lives would be at stake. The gallows loomed as the consequence for failure.

On June 7, shortly after Jefferson returned to Congress, his fellow Virginia delegate Richard Henry Lee offered a resolution:

Resolved: That these United Colonies are, and of right ought to be, free and independent States, that they are absolved from all allegiance to the British Crown, and that all political connection between them and the State of Britain is, and ought to be, totally dissolved.

Although the movement for independence expressed in Lee's resolution was gaining overwhelming support, there were still some delegates who wished to find a path of compromise with Britain. On June 11 Congress postponed a final vote on the resolution and appointed a committee of five delegates to draft a statement presenting to the world the colonies' case for independence. The committee included John Adams, Benjamin Franklin, Robert R. Livingston of New York, Roger Sherman of Connecticut, and Thomas Jefferson.

The committee selected Jefferson to draft the statement on independence. Looking back on these days of 1776, John Adams remembered that Jefferson had been a logical choice. He represented the largest state, Virginia; unlike some of his colleagues, he had few enemies; and he was a superb writer. He began work immediately.

When Jefferson first took lodging in Philadelphia it was on Chestnut Street, at the house of a cabinetmaker named Benjamin Randolph. Jefferson asked Randolph to construct for him a portable mahogany writing desk, lined with green felt. This desk became one of his proudest possessions. Late in his life he gave the desk as a wedding present to his granddaughter. The desk, he told her then, had an important connection to the nation's birthday. Indeed, it was on that desk, closeted in a small room on Market Street (to which he had moved in May 1776) that Jefferson wrote the Declaration of Independence.

When Jefferson sat down at the desk the task was clear—to present in unmistakable, precise language the justification for revolution, for the demand for independence; to write a dignified document that embraced the ideals and hopes of the American people, a document around which they could rally. He succeeded masterfully. The Declaration of Independence contained no grand philosophical arguments with which the colonists were not already familiar. It derived, instead, from Jef-

Congress votes for independence on July 2, 1776. Up to this point, most Americans were still loyal to George III, despite their 14-month war against the British. They had hoped that the colonies' show of fighting spirit would result in the replacement of Britain's hostile ministers with a friendlier regime.

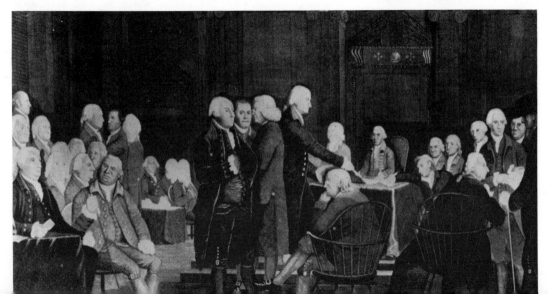

ferson's familiarity with English law, with philosophers such as John Locke, with political arguments he had heard over the years in taverns, pulpits, and courts of law. The polished, memorable phrases surrounded majestically the stinging attacks on the British king. The author appealed to the "Laws of Nature and of Nature's God"; he held up for mankind the right to "life, liberty, and the pursuit of happiness." He held up a proud vision for a new nation.

The committee of five delegates gave the finished draft to Congress as the vote on the Lee motion for independence was about to be called. On July 2 the Congress voted in favor of the motion, in favor of making the American war against the British a war for independence.

The Declaration then came before the Congress. For two and a half days, with its author nervously listening, the delegates debated the document line by line. They made some changes, mostly in style. They struck from the document a statement that faulted the king for allowing the continuation of the African slave trade. Representatives from South Carolina and Georgia, two colonies whose economic stability was highly dependent on slaves, had demanded that the statement be removed. Most of the delegates, it was clear, did not want the thorny issue of slavery to jeopardize the acceptance of the Declaration.

When the delegates had completed their work on the draft, Jefferson felt that the Declaration was a weaker document. He called some of the changes "mutilations." And yet, as the years went by, Jefferson took increasing pride in its authorship, as well he might. Its bold, rounded, inspiring phrases would echo throughout the history of his country.

Late in the afternoon of July 4, 12 of the 13 states approved the Declaration. Only New York's representatives, who had not yet received their instructions from home, failed to vote that day. They made the decision unanimous 11 days later.

The first printed copies of the Declaration were turned out from the shop of John Dunlap, printer, to the Congress on July 5, and the delegates began

> *In general I believe the decisions of the people in a body will be more honest and more disinterested than those of wealthy men.*
> —THOMAS JEFFERSON

to distribute them to the various state assemblies and conventions. On July 19 Congress ordered the Declaration to be written on parchment for formal signature by the delegates. On August 2, John Hancock of Massachusetts, president of the Congress, stepped forward as the first to sign, the other delegates following him according to geographical location of their colony. Eventually, 56 delegates signed, though not all were present on August 2. John Dickinson of Pennsylvania, who still hoped for a peaceful settlement with Britain, refused to sign. Robert R. Livingston, who thought the representatives had been premature in declaring independence, also declined.

Thomas Jefferson now prepared to return to Monticello. As he left Philadelphia, he, along with the other signers of the Declaration of Independence, realized that in the eyes of the British king and the British Parliament, they were all traitors.

Citizens' reactions range from stunned silence to jubilation as they listen to a reading of the Declaration of Independence in July 1776. The Philadelphia block where the document was first read to the public has been known ever since as Independence Square.

3

Return to Virginia

Only 33 years of age, but one of the most prominent political figures in America, Thomas Jefferson returned to his beloved Albemarle County. His future rested, as did the future of all Americans, with the success or failure of the war. But for now, with his family at his side, he could once again be master of Monticello, directing exciting building projects at the estate and experimenting with new agricultural products. More than 100 people—family members, hired workers, and slaves—lived at Monticello. Over 80 of them were slaves.

"All men are created equal," Jefferson had written earlier in the year; all men had the right to life, liberty, and the pursuit of happiness. The author of the Declaration of Independence was profoundly troubled by the condition of the black men, women, and children laboring in servitude at his own plantation and in other establishments in the South. For Thomas Jefferson, the student of philosophy and law, the proponent of human liberty, the institution of slavery was an immense philosophical problem. He never resolved it.

Many times Jefferson advocated ending the slave trade, arguing that it was morally wrong, barbaric, unjust; yet, when he died he owned over 250 slaves.

Southern farm workers planting crops. Jefferson's attitude toward blacks was contradictory. He referred to Negroes as "beings born with equal rights to us," and called slavery "an injustice both barbarous and cruel," but his own Virginia plantation was tended exclusively by slaves.

Thomas Jefferson was eager to reform Virginia's laws, especially those concerning religious freedom. Unusually tolerant for a man of his time, he remarked, "It does me no injury for my neighbor to say there are twenty gods or no god. It neither picks my pocket nor breaks my leg."

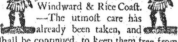

A poster announces a new shipment of "fine, healthy Negroes." In the late 1770s Jefferson came up with a plan for the eventual resettlement in Africa of all children born to slaves; they could be replaced, he said, by free white colonists from Europe. The scheme was quickly rejected by Jefferson's fellow planters.

They built and maintained Monticello, planted his crops, cooked his food, cared for his children. The man who called for the natural right to life and liberty ran advertisements in local newspapers seeking the capture of his runaway slaves. The man who, as a member of the Virginia House of Delegates, supported a law providing for freedom for slaves in Virginia, kept most of his own human property when such a law was finally adopted. The man who on many occasions wrote of the despotism and tyranny of slavery allowed the occasional whipping of some of the captured runaways. The man who attempted to include an antislavery statement in the Declaration of Independence also wrote that he believed blacks were probably inferior to whites, both mentally and physically. Jefferson reportedly treated his slaves well compared to other plantation owners. He developed close personal attachments to some. But they remained his property.

Later, in 1820, when northern and southern states began to battle in the United States Congress over the question of slavery, Jefferson wrote of his fears that the nation would be hopelessly torn apart by the issue. He warned of the dreadful danger ahead. It was "like a fire-bell in the night," filling him with terror. This problem of slavery, he wrote, was like "having the wolf by the ears, and we can neither hold him, nor safely let him go." This was 40 years before the Civil War.

If Jefferson found the issue of slavery perplexing, he nevertheless demonstrated over the years a fierce determination to fight for the rights of those less privileged than himself. Nowhere was this resolve more evident than in his efforts to mold the laws of Virginia.

From the day he returned to Monticello late in 1776, Jefferson worked steadfastly to change what he regarded as a state government too rooted in the past, too much controlled by a handful of wealthy, landed families. At the time Jefferson had been working in the Continental Congress, Virginia's political leaders had been constructing a new constitution for the state, a constitution to replace the old system of British rule under which Virginians had lived for so long. Jefferson was not satisfied with the result.

The philosopher from Monticello considered the revolution against the British only a beginning toward reforming American society. He hoped for a fresh, bold experiment in self-government, a system in which the rights to "life, liberty, and the pursuit of happiness" could be assured for the people, a government that would rule by popular consent. In the new Virginia constitution, which he read upon his return, Jefferson found that little had changed. He charged into a long battle to reshape Virginia's laws. It became a personal crusade.

As a delegate to the Virginia assembly, Jefferson fought successfully for new legislation that made much Virginia land previously controlled by single families for generations, available to greater numbers of people. The land, Jefferson believed, must not be the private domain of the aristocracy, families whose members exercised a power founded not on natural talents, but on birth and inherited possessions. He looked forward to the day when the nation would be filled with small farmers, men of virtue and ability, who acquired their property through achievement, not birthright.

Jefferson also struggled hard for a broad program of public education. "If a nation expects to be ignorant and free in a state of civilization," he wrote, "it expects what never was and never will be." Without an educated public, he believed, society itself would collapse. To provide this broad education, government must accept responsibility. In addition to advocating a state-sponsored educational system, he fought for the building of a free public library and for the special training of intellectually gifted children, regardless of social position. Although not all Jefferson's proposals were adopted by Virginia, his program still stands as a symbol of his determination to establish a system of government responsible to all the people.

Jefferson also fought for full religious freedom. The Anglican church was a powerful force in Virginia. It was supported by state taxes, paid even by members of society who did not accept the church's

RUN away from the subscriber in Albemarle, a Mulatto slave called Sandy, about 35 years of age, his stature is rather low, inclining to corpulence, and his complexion light; he is a shoemaker by trade, in which he uses his left hand principally, can do coarse carpenters work, and is something of a horse jockey; he is greatly addicted to drink, and when drunk is insolent and disorderly, in his conversation he swears much, and in his behaviour is artful and knavish. He took with him a white horse, much scarred with traces, of which it is expected he will endeavour to dispose; he also carried his shoemakers tools, and will probably endeavour to get employment that way. Whoever conveys the said slave to me, in Albemarle, shall have 40 s. reward, if taken up within the county, 4 l. if elsewhere within the colony, and 10 l. if in any other colony, from
THOMAS JEFFERSON.

"Run away from the subscriber in Albemarle," said the advertisement in a Virginia newspaper, was "a Mulatto [part white] slave called Sandy." The advertiser, who offered a reward for the return of the "artful and knavish" Sandy, was Thomas Jefferson.

Those who labor in the earth are the chosen people of God, if ever he had a chosen people, whose breasts He has made His peculiar deposit for substantial and genuine virtue.
—THOMAS JEFFERSON
quoted from his
Notes on the State of Virginia

45

Small, well-kept farms border a colonial turnpike. Jefferson's vision of an ideal country was a republic populated by farmers: a nation where wealth and power would be renounced in favor of simplicity, freedom, and equal opportunity.

> *All persons shall have full and free liberty of religious opinion; nor shall any be compelled to frequent or maintain any religious institution.*
> —THOMAS JEFFERSON
> quoted from his
> "Draft Constitution for Virginia,"
> written in 1776

teachings or participate in its activities. Jefferson vigorously opposed such special privileges. The legitimate powers of government must not extend to religious belief, he insisted. "Millions of innocent men, women, and children, since the introduction of Christianity, have been burnt, tortured, fined, and imprisoned" because governments forced religion on their people. Religious feeling was a personal matter, Jefferson declared, and not within the jurisdiction of civil government. His crusade for religious liberty in Virginia was long and bitter. Not until 1786 did the legislature pass a bill declaring all men free to express their own religious beliefs and engage in their own worship without interference. Jefferson later counted this protracted struggle and resounding victory among his greatest achievements.

In all of these efforts—the fight to open lands to greater numbers of people, the proposals for public education, the battle for religious freedom—Jefferson sought to create the kind of society envisioned in the Declaration of Independence. The stirring phrases in the Declaration—"inalienable rights," "consent of the governed," "all men are created equal"—found expression in Jefferson's determination to establish in Virginia a society he called "truly republican," a society free of the stifling control of the wealthy.

But if Jefferson had forward-looking views concerning these and other aspects of society and politics, there were some areas, in addition to slavery, in which he reflected the dominant, conservative attitudes of most of 18th-century America. He completely distrusted the ability of the working class to participate constructively in politics. Regarding women, Jefferson once observed that they were perhaps "too wise to wrinkle their foreheads with politics."

During Jefferson's three years in Virginia's assembly (1776–1779), the fate of America's revolution rested to a large extent on the backs of the soldiers. Many of these men were underfed, ill-clothed and poorly equipped and were ill-prepared for sloshing through the mud and cold at such places as Morristown, New Jersey, and Valley Forge, Pennsylvania. From his peaceful Monticello vantage point, Jefferson cheered the news of each hard-won American victory. But he also heard gloomy reports of the immense suffering of the American troops, their heavy casualties, woeful lack of rations, and widespread discontent. Despite these difficulties, Jefferson appeared confident that American success was assured, that right would triumph over adversity.

The Marquis de Lafayette (left; 1757–1834) shares the bitterly cold winter of 1777–78 with George Washington and his army at Valley Forge, Pennsylvania. Hungry, unpaid, and unsheltered, the Americans also lacked shoes and uniforms. One officer said his men were so ill-clothed that they were known as "the naked regiment."

The Continental Congress tried to finance the war by issuing paper currency with a total face value of $241.5 million. The money quickly depreciated, and bills soon cost more to print than they would buy. By 1781, "not worth a continental" had become a common expression.

Some of Jefferson's friends, however, could barely hide their resentment of the revolutionary writer from Monticello. Jefferson, they felt, the man who articulated America's yearning for independence, had chosen to remain at home, far removed from national affairs. While Americans were dying in this war, a war in whose beginnings he had been deeply involved, Jefferson was in the Virginia hills planting orange trees, examining lightning bugs, studying eclipses, and adding new deer to his nearby park. A story later circulated that while leading troops in the North, George Washington sarcastically asked, "Where's Jefferson?"

But Jefferson's three years of work in the assembly had been precisely the kind of work of which he felt himself capable. He knew nothing about military affairs or strategies. His battleground would be in public office, his weapon the pen.

In June 1779, the 36-year-old from Monticello was appointed governor of Virginia by the state legislature. He faced a formidable challenge. Virginia lacked money in its treasury and had a poorly supplied militia. A British invasion of the state had just begun.

Unable to defeat the Continental Army under Washington in the North, the British commander-in-chief, Sir Henry Clinton, had decided to strike the Americans in the South. In December 1778 Savannah, Georgia, fell to the British, who were soon attacking the defenses of Charleston, South Carolina. In May 1779, a month before Jefferson took over as governor, a British fleet struck Virginia at Hampton Roads, unleashing its 1,800 troops on the Portsmouth area. They devastated the region, looting and burning several towns and destroying tobacco crops and military supplies. Jefferson and other Virginians knew that the Hampton Roads landing was only the first blow.

Virginia's defense rested mostly on ill-trained, ill-equipped militiamen, farmers who were expected to leave their plows immediately on word of redcoat invasion and rush to fight. As the onslaught of heavily armed British troops continued, the morale of the American militia sagged; some men even joined the enemy. Virginia seemed unable to resist the British forces.

Jefferson worked tirelessly during this period mustering troops and securing supplies, corresponding with military commanders, and helping to devise strategies to hold off the invading force. The odds against the colonial forces were overwhelming.

In January 1781 Benedict Arnold, a former American general who had joined the British, a man who would go down in American history as perhaps its most infamous traitor, led British troops into Richmond, Virginia's new state capital. The invaders set fire to much of the city and forced Jefferson and the government to flee to Charlottesville. British troops poured into the state both by sea and by land, in fearful numbers, overrunning the defenses. Jefferson was himself almost taken prisoner. He escaped capture only by riding through the wooded mountains near Monticello that he had known so well since childhood.

Toward the end of 1781 Jefferson informed the legislature that he did not wish to continue as governor. His training and talents, he said, had not prepared him to oversee a military campaign. His decision caused him much personal pain and considerable political damage. Some Virginians charged that he had been negligent and incompetent, even cowardly, in his handling of the crisis—accusations that would haunt his later political life.

When Jefferson left office the plight of his fellow Virginians was quite grave. He could not have foreseen the tremendous American success that would come later that year. With a French fleet commanded by Admiral Count François de Grasse assisting American troops led by the Marquis de Lafayette and Baron von Steuben, and with much of Washington's army rushing in from the north, the revolutionists launched a major assault against Lord Cornwallis's British troops at Yorktown, Virginia. After severe hammering by allied siege artillery, Cornwallis surrendered. British troops laid down their arms as their bands played "The World Turned Upside Down."

Benedict Arnold (1741–1801), the American general whose name became a synonym for "traitor," had been a military hero in the battles of Quebec and Saratoga. Passed over for promotion, the embittered Arnold sold his services to the enemy, became a British general, and moved to London after the war.

The Marquis de Lafayette, an idealistic and wealthy young Frenchman, was a fervent believer in the cause of American liberty. Commissioned a major general in the Continental Army after he arrived in a ship equipped at his own expense, Lafayette proved himself a brave, popular, and capable officer.

If Thomas Jefferson had remained in office, perhaps the victory at Yorktown would have saved his reputation as governor. As it was, he returned to Monticello, the assaults on his performance as governor leaving him a bitter man. He vowed never to return to public office, having "retired to my farm, my family and books from which I think nothing will ever more separate me."

Jefferson's time away from the public stage gave him the opportunity to work on a project that eventually resulted in his only published book, a sweeping intellectual adventure entitled *Notes on the State of Virginia.* First appearing in France in 1825, the book is a remarkable document, reflecting the depth and breadth of Jefferson's intellect and philosophy. He wrote about the towns, rivers, mountains, climate, and plants of his native state. He described in detail Virginia's history, laws, religions, economy, and customs. Most of all, he showed why so many people in later years hailed him as the leading American contributor to the Enlightenment, an 18th-century intellectual movement whose adherents proclaimed the supremacy of reason. He was philosopher and scientist, political theorist and historian. The book ensured for Jefferson an established scientific and literary following on both sides of the Atlantic.

On September 6, 1782, deep personal tragedy struck Thomas Jefferson. He lost his beloved Martha. She had never fully recovered from the birth of her sixth child the previous May. Jefferson's oldest daughter, Martha, whom the family now called Patsy, remembered her father caring for his wife as she lingered through the fall. When not at her bedside, he did his writing in a small adjacent room. Her death caused Jefferson immense grief. "He fell into a state of insensibility from which it was feared he would not revive," Patsy wrote later. Jefferson stayed in his room for weeks, pacing to and fro, only lying down when completely exhausted. "When he at last left his room, he rode out, and from that time he was incessantly on horseback, rambling about the mountain, on the least frequented roads, and just as often through the woods. In those melancholy rambles I was his constant companion—a solitary witness to many a burst of grief." On a paper found in Jefferson's pocketbook after his death are these words: "There is a time in human suffering when exceeding sorrows are but like snow falling on an iceberg." Thomas Jefferson never married again.

At age 39, Jefferson was now a widower with three young children—Patsy, Mary, and Lucy Elizabeth, the baby born in May, who would die two years later. Without Martha, Monticello was now heavy with memories. Jefferson was unable to work, burdened, as he said later, with a "gloom unbrightened with one cheerful expectation."

Martha Jefferson (1748–1782) died at 33, leaving her husband inconsolable. For a time, he later wrote, he doubted his ability to carry on without "the cherished companion of my life, in whose affections, unabated on both sides, I had lived the last ten years in unchequered happiness."

Symbolizing the defeat at Yorktown of the British army commanded by General Charles Cornwallis (1738–1805), Brigadier Charles O'Hara presents his sword to George Washington's deputy, General Benjamin Lincoln (1733–1810), on October 19, 1781. Yorktown signaled the ultimate triumph of the Americans, but the conflict dragged on for another year and a half.

4

Back to the National Arena

What country before ever existed a century and a half without a rebellion? The tree of liberty must be refreshed from time to time with the blood of patriots and tyrants. It is its natural manure.
—THOMAS JEFFERSON

Jefferson had left the governorship of Virginia determined never to return to public office. However, Martha's death and a request from Congress in November 1782 changed his mind. He was appointed one of three Americans to meet with the British in Paris for peace negotiations. The other two members of the delegation, John Adams and Benjamin Franklin, were already in Europe.

Jefferson left immediately for Philadelphia, where he was to embark for France. When he arrived in December, Jefferson found that the trip had been postponed because the ship that was to carry him to Europe was icebound. For three months, Jefferson scurried around Philadelphia, collecting books and maps, studying, and meeting with members of Congress. Finally, the trip became unnecessary when a peace treaty was signed in Paris on February 3, 1783. The American War of Independence was over. Perhaps it was fitting that Thomas Jefferson was not in Europe but in Philadelphia, where he had written the declaration that helped to start it all.

Louis XVI (1754—1793), who ruled France at the time of the American Revolution, was sympathetic to the colonists' struggle for independence from Britain, France's traditional enemy. Ironically, he lost his crown—and his head—during the revolution that swept his own country between 1789 and 1793.

When Jefferson took his place in Congress in 1783, the nation's currency was a hodgepodge of state-issued and foreign bills and coins. Jefferson recommended a unified monetary system based on units of 10; the decimal system was eventually adopted in the United States.

Jefferson's proposal for the Northwest Territory—the parcel of land that was to become Ohio, Indiana, Illinois, Michigan, and Wisconsin—provided that any part of the area could be admitted to the union as a state as soon as it had as many free inhabitants as the smallest of the original 13 states.

Versailles was among the architectural marvels that fascinated Jefferson when he arrived in Paris in 1784. King Louis XIII (1601–1643) had begun construction of the magnificent palace and its elaborate gardens in 1627.

The war's conclusion triggered in Jefferson a new enthusiasm for public life. In 1783 he was chosen as a delegate to the national Congress. Within a few months he produced one of the most significant documents issued in this period—a plan for the addition of new states beyond the Appalachian Mountains.

The original colonies, now independent from Britain, had joined together in a confederation of states governed by the Congress. Jefferson's plan provided for the orderly addition of more states to the confederation; it sought to prevent uncontrolled expansion by the settlers filling up the lands west of the Appalachian Mountains. These new states-to-be, Jefferson believed, could bring greater strength and stability to the nation if their growth and development could be properly regulated.

Always the spokesman for the new American nation, Jefferson, in his plan for the western regions, was seeking a way to harness America's resources for the common good. Many of his ideas later found their way into the Northwest Ordinance of 1787, the act that finally became the approved plan of Congress for westward expansion.

In May 1784 the Congress appointed Jefferson to a three-man commission to negotiate treaties of commerce with European states. Again, Benjamin Franklin and John Adams would be co-members. And again their destination would be Paris. This time, however, his ship would sail. Jefferson, a person of refinement, culture, and learning, a man

who already knew something of Europe through books and through long, late-night conversations with men who had lived there, would finally see it firsthand.

He sailed from Boston, taking Patsy with him and leaving his two youngest daughters with their aunt in Virginia. Paris in 1784 was a teeming city of about 600,000 people, a metropolis graced with magnificent buildings, opera houses, art galleries, and beautiful gardens. Bookstalls lined the banks of the Seine River, providing endless hours of quiet browsing through volumes of ancient history and philosophy. Paris was a city where Jefferson's craving for knowledge could be satisfied.

He wasted no time in seeking to acquaint himself with all that Paris had to offer. He treated himself to an exhilarating tour of the city, walking the centuries-old streets, glorying in the fabulous restaurants, satisfying his cultural curiosity, and shopping for books, clothes, engravings, and assorted trinkets. He was particularly excited by the fabulous architecture and the newest inventions. He took notes on wine vintages, plants, birds,

Lafayette had hoped to introduce Jefferson to such Paris landmarks as Notre Dame Cathedral, but the young hero of the American Revolution sailed for Philadelphia just as the Virginian left for France. He urged his American friend, however, to regard his house "as a second home," gallantly adding, "anything that is mine is entirely at your disposal."

A Paris crowd cheers a revolutionary speaker near the king's palace in 1789. Enthusiastic about the oncoming French Revolution, Jefferson believed it would provide "resurrection to a new life" for a people that had been "ground to dust by the abuses of the governing powers."

The lot of the French peasant, "loaded with misery by kings, nobles, and priests," made a powerful impression on Jefferson. "My God!" he said in a letter to a friend, "how little do my countrymen know what precious blessings they are in possession of, and which no other people on earth enjoy."

cathedrals, sculpture, and monuments. He even wrote several pages on the making of Parmesan cheese.

But he also saw poverty and much misery among the French people. He blamed it on the curse of bad government, a curse that made 19 million of the 20 million people in France "more wretched, more accursed in every circumstance of human existence than the most conspicuously wretched individuals of the whole United States." France, this country of kings and priests and noblemen, of wealth and pomp and artistic achievement, was a country in which most people lived in degrading poverty.

Jefferson stayed in France for five years, much longer than he had first planned. In addition to his role as trade negotiator, Congress in 1785 appointed him minister to France to succeed Franklin who, at age 79, had decided to return home. Jefferson worked hard in these years to build up increasing trade between France and the United States and to find ways to help his country pay off the large debt to the French accumulated during the American War of Independence.

It was also during these years that the French Revolution erupted, a revolution in which Jefferson recognized many of the same political forces that had led to the American insurrection. Indeed, many of his French friends looked to Jefferson for advice. Because of his sensitive diplomatic position, Jefferson could not speak out publicly on the issues facing the French at this critical time. Privately, however, he talked about the importance of representative government and guarantees of individual rights, and the necessity of removing some of the aristocratic privileges holding down the great mass of French people. The French were divided, Jefferson said, between the few vicious wolves and the great herds of sheep. He did not believe, however, that the French "sheep" were quite ready to engineer the kind of political convulsion that had shaken his own country.

Nevertheless, by the time Jefferson returned to America in the fall of 1789, the French had in place a new national assembly and had adopted the social philosophy of the *Declaration of the Rights of Man and Citizen*, a document similar in tone and spirit to the one Jefferson had composed in America over a decade earlier. Jefferson later

A French engraving shows Louis XVI generously distributing money to the grateful poor; reality in the France of Jefferson's time was, however, quite different. Jefferson was appalled by the callous attitude of the French aristocracy toward the misery in which most of the nation's population lived.

The *Declaration of the Rights of Man* outlined the principles of political equality and liberty that had animated the French Revolution. It was drafted by Lafayette, who had returned to France inspired by the American Declaration of Independence.

began to see the French Revolution as an extension of the American, and he expressed the hope that the French would ultimately prove to have written the "first chapter in the history of European liberty."

While Jefferson was in France, political events back in his own country were taking a significant turn. Led by Jefferson's friend and fellow Virginian, James Madison, a drive for reforming America's confederation government was moving forward. Madison and others were convinced that the existing government of independent states was not able to deal effectively with the growing problems of nationhood.

Under this confederation government, the states were relatively independent. The national government could not tax and was generally unable to establish essential commercial policy with foreign nations. The government also found it difficult to establish a strong national military force to protect the country. In addition, many of the states seemed to be on the brink of economic disaster.

One sign of the country's economic woes was the condition of its farmers. Racked by poverty, many were thrown in jail for debt and had their farms confiscated. In 1786 some of them fought back. Led by a former Continental army captain named Daniel Shays, a group of farmers started a minor rebellion against the authorities in Massachusetts. Although easily put down by state troops, the uprising made many leaders across the country shudder as they imagined an increasing number of such incidents. Shays's Rebellion had the effect of making the need for a strong central government seem even more urgent.

In France, Jefferson followed these developments with much interest. Shays's Rebellion had not mortified him nearly as much as it had some other leading Americans. There was something noble, he thought, about the people rolling up their sleeves to take on established authority. Although not a man to condone mob rule, Jefferson nevertheless respected the people's right to resist their government. "I like a little rebellion now and then. It is like a storm in the atmosphere," he once said.

Early in the drive for a revision of America's government, Jefferson, from his vantage point in France, had been skeptical. He feared that a powerful central government would be unduly restrictive, even oppressive, and he disliked the prospect of a strong executive. He wanted a written "bill of rights," a guarantee of such fundamental personal liberties as freedom of speech. But Jefferson also saw the need to strengthen the nation, to make it more economically and militarily secure.

Led by James Madison and Alexander Hamilton, a young lawyer from New York, Congress issued a formal call to the states for a constitutional convention to be held in Philadelphia beginning in May 1787. Another Virginian, the squire of Gunston Hall, George Mason, wrote to his son, "The Eyes of

The 1786–87 rebellion led by Daniel Shays (1747–1825) and Job Shattuck delighted the British, who said it proved the Americans incapable of self-government. It alarmed most of the American leaders, but Jefferson reacted with serenity. "The tree of liberty," he commented, "must be refreshed from time to time with the blood of patriots and tyrants."

the United States are turned upon this Assembly." Other eyes were also focusing intently. When Congress announced that the proceedings were to be held in secret, Jefferson wrote, "I am sorry they began their deliberations by so abominable a precedent as that of tying up the tongues of their members."

After weeks of intense debate in the close confines of Philadelphia's Independence Hall, almost insufferable in the sweltering summer heat, the delegates finally agreed on a new constitution. "We the people of the United States," it began, "in order to form a more perfect Union. . . ." On receiving a copy of the Constitution, Jefferson again warned of the dangers of a strong central government: "Our Convention," he charged, "has been too much interested by the insurrection of Massachusetts." Some men had a great fear of the breakdown of law and order and the horrors of civil uprising; Jefferson had a greater fear of the strong arm of centralized authority.

The new Constitution, which provided for a president and for stronger federal control in matters of defense, taxation, and foreign relations, still worried Jefferson. Nevertheless, as the people in the

Independence Hall was the birthplace of the U.S. Constitution, hammered out in 1787 by 55 delegates from 12 states. (Rhode Island declined to attend.) The delegates were surprisingly young: five were less than 30 years old, and only four—including the 81-year-old Benjamin Franklin—were more than 60 years old.

states began to decide whether to adopt the new constitution, he made it clear to Madison and others that he favored it. The strong union of the states and the promise of greater mutual protection and support outweighed the defects he saw in the proposed government. To Jefferson, the survival of the nation remained the supreme concern. He still vigorously argued for a bill of rights, later pushed through the federal Congress by Madison. He argued that a president's term should be limited, thereby avoiding the possibility of a kinglike executive ascending to power. However, when he looked at the democratic process that had brought about the new Consitution, his concern softened and he glowed with national pride: "Happily for us that when we find our constitutions defective and insufficient, to secure the happiness of our people, we can assemble with all the coolness of philosophers, and set it to rights, while every other nation on earth must have recourse to arms." Jefferson the revolutionary was now Jefferson the constitutionalist.

To catalogue the areas of his explorations is to list most of the principal categories of knowledge—law, government, history, mathematics, architecture, medicine, agriculture, languages and literature, education, music, philosophy, religion, and almost every branch of the natural sciences from astronomy through meteorology to zoology.
—JULIAN P. BOYD
modern American philosopher
and art critic

5
The Secretary of State

Jefferson returned to the United States in November 1789. It was an historic time. A few months earlier George Washington, a man almost godlike in the eyes of his countrymen, had taken the oath of office as the nation's first president. In his inaugural address at Federal Hall in New York, Washington spoke of the United States as rising under the guidance of Heaven, a nation having "the sacred fire of liberty."

As the country now started on its new experiment in government, few American leaders were completely satisfied with the Constitution. At the federal convention two years earlier, the discussions had been like a game of dice, Benjamin Franklin said, with many players of different backgrounds, interests, and prejudices, all debating, arguing, compromising, and arguing some more. Madison told Jefferson that the bringing together of all the clashing interests—the northern states with the southern, small states with the large, farmers with shippers—had been a task more difficult than any he had ever imagined.

And now the new government under the Constitution was to begin. As President Washington searched for the best men to assist him in the difficult job that lay ahead, he looked to Thomas

After five years in Europe, Jefferson was eager to go home, but rumors that America had undergone "a great spiritual change" made him somewhat apprehensive. "I know only the Americans of the year 1784," he wrote a friend. "They tell me this is to be much a stranger to those of 1789."

Martha Jefferson Randolph (1772–1836) received a good education, but her father expected her to use it only to advance "domestic happiness": The business of women, Jefferson counseled, was "to soothe and calm the minds of their husbands." Following her adored father's bidding, Martha became a dutiful wife, housekeeper, and mother.

George Washington was an almost mythological figure, even in his own lifetime. Parson Weems's 1800 best-seller, *Life of Washington*, was the source of many popular but fictitious anecdotes, including the one about young George's confession ("I can't tell a lie, Pa") that he had chopped down his father's favorite cherry tree.

Jefferson. He asked Jefferson to be the nation's first secretary of state.

Washington's letter offering Jefferson this post placed Virginia's distinguished son in a difficult position. He did not want the job. Satisfied with the work he had done in France, Jefferson had planned to return to Paris after his visit to Virginia. Assuming the office of secretary of state also promised to be an administrative nightmare, he believed. The fact that the State Department offices were located in New York, a city that lacked the charm and grace of Paris, did little to increase his interest. After further encouragement from both Washington and Madison, however, Jefferson finally accepted the job, saying that he must bow down to "the will of my country."

Before Jefferson left for New York, his eldest daughter, Martha, married her second cousin, Thomas Mann Randolph, a well-educated and wealthy man with appropriate family connections. Jefferson was delighted with the match. A sensitive woman with an impressive intellect and many talents, Martha could look forward to the typical life of an aristocratic planter's wife. So could her sister Mary, who in 1797 became the wife of John Wayles Eppes, later a United States congressman. Most other life's paths were closed for America's women, even for the daughters of Thomas Jefferson. Professional fields—law, politics, the clergy, the military—were for men only two centuries ago.

As he left for New York, Jefferson rode by horse to Alexandria, Virginia, and then, because of heavy snow, by stage to Philadelphia, where he visited the dying Benjamin Franklin. The new secretary of state arrived in New York in late March 1790 to begin his duties.

Jefferson soon met with Washington, for whom he had great respect. He also met his new colleagues: Secretary of War Henry Knox, Attorney General Edmund Randolph, and Secretary of the Treasury Alexander Hamilton. Jefferson's first meetings with Hamilton were friendly. The two men, however, would soon become fierce political antagonists.

Born in the Leeward Islands in the West Indies, Hamilton was more than a decade younger than Jefferson. Brilliant and ambitious, he served in the Revolution, first as commander of an artillery unit and then as Washington's secretary. Hamilton loved all things military. He once remarked that Julius Caesar was his favorite character in history, a statement that appalled Jefferson, who respected men of ideas, not of the sword. Hamilton also served in the Continental Congress and was one of the leading supporters of the Constitutional Convention, which he attended as a delegate from New York. A vigorous, articulate advocate for a strong central government, Hamilton greatly distrusted the instincts of the masses and favored an increasing federal authority in all matters of public policy. A strong government, he believed, was the proper agent of order and stability.

When Hamilton took over the reins of the treasury department as its first secretary, he faced an enormous challenge. He needed to establish the young nation's credit on a sound basis. The government owed large sums not only to the foreign powers that had aided America in the Revolutionary War but to individuals at home as well. Hamilton argued strongly that the federal government should assume responsibility for the entire body of debts, including that amassed by the various states during the war. He proposed to raise the money through taxes on goods imported from other countries and through an excise, a tax on the manufacture and sale of goods within the United States. One of these excises, a tax on whiskey, especially hurt small backwoods farmers who cultivated grain used in the making of whiskey. In addition to these measures, Hamilton also pushed for a national bank that would act as the government's depository and as a central control on the operation of state banks.

By the time Jefferson reached New York in early 1790, much of Hamilton's plan was already in place. Jefferson objected almost immediately. Although he went to work aggressively on foreign policy matters, the true business of the secretary of state, a great amount of his time and energy was soon

Alexander Hamilton (1755–1804) was appointed secretary of the treasury in 1789. Treasury was then the most important and powerful of the federal departments, responsible not only for raising and spending government funds, but for operating lighthouses, land surveys, and the postal service. By 1800, it employed over half of all federal employees.

Henry Knox (1750–1806) was the first U.S. secretary of war. A close friend and adviser of Washington, he had served as a brigadier general in the Continental Army and as commander of the military academy at West Point, which he helped establish in 1779.

James Madison (1751–1836) was a close friend and loyal political ally of Jefferson, whom he succeeded as president in 1808 (he served until 1817). Madison was the only U.S. president to face enemy gunfire while in office: He led an artillery battery during the British invasion of Washington in the War of 1812.

Jefferson's mind did not move in a world of narrow circumstances; it did not confine itself to the conditions of a single race or a single continent.
—WOODROW WILSON
president of the United States
(1913–21)

directed toward opposing Hamilton's economic policies. This national taxation to pay back the war debts, Jefferson argued, was an unfair burden on farmers, tradesmen, and others in American society with little money. Here was an example of government again becoming the oppressor. It had no right to levy such taxes. The country had rid itself of British tyranny only to be saddled with self-inflicted tyranny.

Hamilton and Jefferson began to quarrel over many issues, all of them revolving around the question of governmental power and the degrees to which the country was to be controlled by its national authorities. Hamilton, in one of his early statements of policy, claimed that when the people formed the government, they gave it the right to take whatever measures were necessary for the common good, unless such measures seemed to contradict the spirit of the Constitution. Jefferson, on the other hand, argued that all powers not specifically given to the national government by the Constitution were reserved for the states and the people. Hamilton insisted that the Constitution gave broad powers to the central government, while Jefferson argued that it gave only limited power. From these fundamental philosophical differences arose the nation's first two political parties.

On the one side, the two principal leaders were Jefferson and his close associate and fellow Virginian, James Madison, now a member of the first federal congress under the new government. The men who aligned themselves with Jefferson and Madison soon became known as "Republicans." On the other side, the leaders were Hamilton, John Adams, and Washington, whose decisions during these first years of his administration usually favored Hamilton's philosophy. These men and their followers became known as "Federalists." In the early years of the new government, the two parties were loosely organized; some political leaders even denied their existence out of fear that political strife would jeopardize the government. But as the months passed it was clear that a deep split did, indeed, exist.

Both sides had their own newspapers which churned out issue after issue of vicious, backbiting articles attacking their opponents. The *National Gazette*, run by Philip Freneau, a poet and classmate of Madison at Princeton, began to insult Hamilton and his followers, calling them power-hungry, rich snobs bent on snatching the government from the people.

The Federalist paper, the *Gazette of the United States*, charged that Jefferson and his associates were promoting principles dangerous to the security of the nation. The Federalist paper glowingly called Washington "His Excellence" and "His Highness," terms at which Jefferson sneered. The use of these titles, he believed, was further proof of the Federalist desire to return the country to a virtual monarchy. Washington's own practice of wearing black velvet clothes, powdered wig, yellow gloves,

Both the Federalists and the Republicans employed biting satire to mock their opponents. In this 1793 anti-Republican cartoon, the shabbily dressed, pistol-armed man in the center says, "Damn Governments. I shall never be worth a dollar as long as there's any government at all."

A Peep into the Antifederal Club

and a long sword, as well as his love of hosting ceremonies full of pomp and splendor, made Jefferson distrustful of the direction in which the president seemed to be moving. The nation had just fought to eliminate the power of King George III of England in America; the last thing Jefferson wanted to see was the coronation of his own country's King George I.

Political passions began to seethe. Social functions often became the scene of hysterical speech-making. Old friends, divided now over politics, crossed streets to avoid meeting. Fights erupted, not only in taverns and alleys, but in the Congress itself.

In 1781 the United States government moved its headquarters from New York to Philadelphia, much to Jefferson's delight. For Jefferson, Philadelphia was America's Paris. He took pleasure in its libraries; its American Philosophical Society, where he spent many days discussing the latest scientific discoveries; its Natural History Museum, where he marveled at "a vast variety of monsters of the earth . . . and fowls of the air"; its botanical garden; and its theater.

Philadelphia would not be the permanent capital of the United States. The Congress had already approved a site on the Potomac River near Georgetown, between Virginia and Maryland. Jefferson favored the site because of its location midway between the northern and southern states. As usual, given his many interests, Jefferson had suggestions to offer—on the location and design of the buildings, on the purchase of property, on place names, even on the machinery to be used for cutting and polishing building stone. He also suggested that the city restrict the height of buildings, a practice that Washington, D.C., still follows. The idea was Jefferson's. Where did he get it? Paris, of course!

Jefferson's inclination to support the French became an increasingly strong issue on the political battlefield. In 1792 the seemingly endless war between Britain and France erupted once again. Although the United States declared neutrality, the

Philip Freneau (1752–1832), editor of the rabidly anti-Federalist newspaper, *National Gazette*, was known as "the Poet of the American Revolution." A ship captain as well as a satirist, he wrote a popular verse account, "The British Prison Ship," of his capture at sea during the Revolution.

two political parties had decidedly different views on which country, Britain or France, could better serve America's own interests. Jefferson, Madison, and the other Republicans were generally hostile to Britain and utterly disdainful of the British system of government. They were determined to move the United States away from British commercial domination. Jefferson continually pushed to open new markets for the United States to lessen its dependency on trade with Britain.

Hamilton and the Federalists saw things differently. They worked toward better relations with Britain, the leading trading partner of the United States. They admired the stability of the British government and, in many ways, tried to fashion the United States in the British image. Federalist political figures tended to see themselves as a natural aristocracy of leaders, much like the British nobility.

The Federalists had to overcome the national sympathy many Americans had for the French who, after all, were so vital in helping overthrow British control of the American colonies. The French Revolution, with its wholesale executions, eroded some of that sympathy, and the Federalists began to spread malicious and effective propaganda about the French people, their customs, and their principal religion, Catholicism. To most Federalists the

Nature intended me for the tranquil pursuits of science, by rendering them my supreme delight. But the enormities of the times in which I have lived, have forced me to take part in resisting them, and to commit myself on the boisterous ocean of political passions.
—THOMAS JEFFERSON

Elegantly dressed Philadelphians are driven past the University of Pennsylvania. Philadelphia, which Jefferson regarded as America's most cultured city, was the capital of the United States from 1790 to 1800.

word "French" became a synonym for "bad" or "odious."

As for Jefferson, his enthusiasm for the French Revolution and his support of the French in their struggle against Britain had remained strong. An episode loomed ahead, however, that would create much embarrassment.

In the spring of 1793 the French ambassador, Edmond Genêt, arrived in the United States. A flamboyant spokesman for the ideals of his country's revolution—"liberty, equality, and fraternity" —Genêt was looking for help in France's war against the British. He reached Philadelphia just after Washington had declared the United States neutral. Genêt was furious. The ingratitude of the Americans, he fumed, was shocking. So soon after their own war they were now turning their backs on their French allies! Grumbling that President Washington was a fraud, that he was posing as the champion of liberty while knifing it in the back, Genêt stirred up many Republican sympathizers in the United States. Thousands jammed the streets in protest meetings; some overzealous individuals shouted that George Washington deserved the same treatment meted out to the French king—the loss of his head. Politics were beginning to seem dangerous in the United States.

Jefferson was in turn infuriated by the outspokenness of the French representative. Genêt's visit had been a disaster, creating just the kind of political unrest that gave support to the Federalist's anti-French claims. "Never in my opinion," Jefferson wrote, "was so calamitous an appointment made, as that of the present minister of France here." Genêt was "hot-headed, all imagination, no judgment, disrespectful, and even indecent towards the President." Jefferson asked the French government to recall Genêt and send a new minister. In France, however, new leaders had seized power and were executing their political enemies. Genêt now feared the loss of his own head if he returned. Although he had lost all authority to deal with the United States on behalf of France, although he had done much damage to French-American relations,

Edmond Genêt (right; 1763–1834) is presented to Washington in 1793. Before he met the president, Genêt had paid for the outfitting of American privateers (private warships) to attack British vessels. Washington, who had pledged his nation's neutrality in the war between France and Britain, was furious.

Genêt was allowed to remain in the United States, where he lived a long life as a farmer in New York.

Thoroughly disappointed over the Genêt affair and with the drift of national affairs, weary of public life, Jefferson decided to leave the cabinet. In his resignation letter Jefferson was gracious, assuring Washington that in retirement he was taking with him a "lively sense of the President's goodness, and would continue gratefully to remember it." Although disgusted by many of Washington's political instincts, Jefferson maintained a cordial relationship with him.

"I am to be liberated from the hated occupations of politics," Jefferson wrote as he left Philadelphia. Retiring to the warm company of relatives and friends and to his farm and his books would be an enormous relief. "I have my house to build, my family to form, and to watch for the happiness of those who labor for mine." He wrote his daughter Martha in 1792 that soon "we will sow our cabbages together." Monticello beckoned.

Monticello, an especially graceful and handsome home for 18th-century America, made a strong impression on its visitors. "Mr. Jefferson," wrote a cultured Frenchman who had fought alongside Lafayette, "is the first American who has consulted the fine arts to know how he should shelter himself from the weather."

6

An Uneasy Retirement

Thomas Jefferson entered retirement with a vengeance. For a time on his beloved hill, he did not even subscribe to a national newspaper, bragging about his temporary ignorance of national affairs. He did stay somewhat informed through correspondence, and he took time to read some of the local papers, but he was now content to be the gentleman farmer. He spent hours riding over his land on horseback, reading, tinkering with labor-saving devices for the estate, and visiting neighbors.

Jefferson was now 50 years old, graying but still trim. Except for wine at dinner, he did not drink or smoke. Most days he stayed out of doors, his ruddy skin freckling in the sun. He built a small nail factory which employed a dozen young slaves. For the planting fields he developed a plow that would lift and turn soil more easily. He experimented with methods of crop rotation and other farming techniques, even joking to Washington about a "certain essence of dung, one pint of which would manure an acre." "I cherish tranquility too much," he said, "to suffer political things to enter my mind at all."

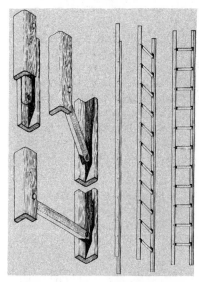

Fascinated by equipment that folded up when not in use, Jefferson designed this wall-mounted ladder, as well as a collapsible camp stool. He also built the first inflatable life-preserver, dumbwaiter, and swivel chair, which his Federalist opponents mockingly called "Mr. Jefferson's whirligig." He never patented his inventions.

Jefferson was neither a speechmaker nor a military hero, but he was popular, perhaps because he expressed the simplicity and positive outlook of everyday Americans. His political goal, he wrote in 1802, was to prove that his countrymen were ready for "a government founded not on the fears and follies of man, but in his reason."

Federalist John Jay (1745–1829) was the first chief justice of the U.S. Supreme Court. Although war was prevented by the 1794 treaty he negotiated with the British, the Republicans—Jefferson included—saw the treaty's signing as a "humiliating" American defeat.

Jefferson's denial of all matters political did not come from the soul. The man was still very much interested in the affairs of government. He complained to friends that the ordinary man of the plow and of the town in his native state knew virtually nothing about national affairs. He wrote to Madison that perhaps the people of the country were not prepared either to approve or disapprove of their government. It amazed him that the raging political fights in Philadelphia were to his neighbors much like news from a foreign country.

However much he occupied himself with agriculture and architecture and his books, however much he was disgusted by the grasping, greedy intrigues of politicians, Jefferson was excited by the public battle, challenged by it all. He could never rest long at Monticello, even with its comforts.

Two political events in 1794 put Jefferson in a combative mood. In July some debt-ridden farmers from western Pennsylvania took up arms and rebelled against the collection of the whiskey taxes.

The British, who had captured Fort Ticonderoga (below) in 1780, abandoned it after the Revolution, but they continued to occupy seven Northwest Territory forts. These outposts reverted to the United States under the terms of Jay's Treaty, which opened the gates for the nation's westward expansion.

George Washington in retirement at Mount Vernon. Many scholars view Washington as an underrated president. "His unique place in history," wrote Samuel Eliot Morison, "rests not only on his superb leadership in war and on his wise administration of the federal government; but even more on his integrity, good judgment, and magnanimity."

President Washington ordered the rebels to return home and called for 15,000 volunteers to quell the uprising. Hamilton and Washington rushed to the scene, Hamilton calling the incident "treason against society, against liberty, against everything that ought to be dear to a free, enlightened, and prudent people."

Although the minor insurrection ended without loss of life, it struck fear into most Federalists, just as Shays's Rebellion in Massachusetts had done earlier. In Federalist eyes this kind of uncontrolled human rabble, uncommitted to the good of the nation, was a menace that might tear apart the government. Such disorder, such attempts at mob rule, must be crushed. In Washington's yearly message to Congress, he denounced the growth of certain "democratic" groups that posed a threat to the country.

Jefferson was outraged by the arrogance of the Federalists in attacking lower-class citizens who were demonstrating against real injustices committed against them. The Pennsylvania "whiskey boys," he claimed, were not such a threat that Washington and his government should have mo-

Aaron Burr (1756–1836), Jefferson's running mate on the 1796 Republican ticket, worked hard to defeat Federalist presidential candidate John Adams. Adams won anyway, Jefferson became vice-president, and Burr returned to his New York law practice. The constitutional method that permitted rival parties to share the administration was changed by Amendment XII in 1804.

We shall never give up our Union, the last anchor of our hope and that alone which is to prevent this heavenly country from becoming an arena of gladiators.

—THOMAS JEFFERSON

bilized an army. The greater evil was not in the protest demonstration but in the "infernal excise law," a tax that should not have been enacted in the first place.

If the so-called Whiskey Rebellion reignited Jefferson's political fires, the Jay Treaty set them blazing. Even though the War of Independence had ended, the British still held some forts on American land across the Allegheny Mountains. Also, British ships were continuing to harass American ships on the high seas. For these reasons a new war between the United States and Britain now seemed possible, and Washington dispatched John Jay to Britain to negotiate a treaty.

Jay did bring back a treaty. Under it, the British agreed to evacuate the occupied forts. The United States, however, agreed to a number of trade concessions that Jefferson and other Republicans felt badly weakened United States independence. It was an American surrender to British power and influence by the pro-British Federalists, Jefferson charged. The Jay Treaty, he wrote to a friend, made him feel as if he were aboard a ship that had been seized by a pirate and run into an enemy's port.

In September 1796 George Washington wrote a farewell address that was first published in Philadelphia. The nation's first president had decided to step down after two terms. "It will be worthy of a free, enlightened, and, at no distant period, a great nation," he declared, "to give mankind the magnanimous and too novel example of a people always guided by an exalted justice and benevolence. . . ." The theme of the address was unity and nationhood, a coming together of north and south, the discarding of political intrigue and jealousy. But as Washington left Philadelphia for his Mount Vernon plantation on the Potomac River, there was little unity in the country, and certainly no appreciable reduction of political infighting. The campaign to elect the next president of the United States was now the issue at the center of the political stage. One of the principal actors was a gentleman farmer from Virginia; the other his crusty, erudite Revolutionary War friend from Massachusetts.

John Adams, Washington's vice-president, indicated early his desire to take over the presidential reins. Widely admired, relatively untainted by the battle raging between Jefferson and Hamilton, John Adams was an extraordinarily intelligent man, dedicated to the best interests of the nation as he saw them. He stood the greatest chance of any Federalist to succeed Washington.

For the Republicans, the choice was either James Madison or Jefferson. Each wanted the other to run. "The little spice of ambition which I had in my younger days has long since evaporated," Jefferson announced when asked to try for the office. Madison, his younger Virginia colleague and friend, persisted. Jefferson was the logical choice—principal spokesman for the Republican party, possessor of an almost legendary reputation both in the United States and abroad, generally popular, enormously respected.

The master of Monticello never did give Madison and his Republican allies his definite consent, but he became their candidate nonetheless. Led by Madison, Aaron Burr, a political enemy of Hamilton from New York, and others, the Republicans began an intensive newspaper and pamphlet campaign that presented Jefferson as the virtuous defender of the people's rights and the Federalist Adams as a creature of money and privilege. The Federalists returned the fire, attacking Jefferson as an opponent of union, a man of no religion, a foe of George Washington, a puppet of France, a dreamy philosopher unsuited to lead a country.

From his hilltop home Jefferson sat back and let the campaign unfold. He once remarked that the extreme flattery of his friends and the vicious attacks hurled by his opponents made him an almost fictitious character.

When the vote was tallied, Adams won narrowly, carrying all of the northern states. Jefferson received the second-highest vote total for president. Because of the electoral rules that existed at the time, he became vice-president. The country now had a Federalist president and a Republican vice-president.

John Adams became president in 1797. Although he was a shrewd political observer, ("Washington got the reputation of being a great man," he said of his predecessor, "because he kept his mouth shut"), he was an uneasy administrator. Benjamin Franklin said he was "always honest, often great, but sometimes mad."

7

Vice-President

In February 1797 Jefferson was once again on his way to Philadelphia, a journey he had made many times before. The new vice-president soon met with the new president. It was a warm reunion, rekindling the mutual respect they had shared since the early days of the Revolution. Although they held opposing views, especially regarding the relationship of the United States with France and Britain, the two had for each other none of the personal hatred that so characterized the American political scene in the 1790s.

This spirit of friendship was evident at the inauguration. As John Adams rose to address a huge crowd in the hall of Congress, he looked to his right, where sat the two distinguished Virginians with whom he shared so many memories—the retiring president and the new vice-president. Their appearance together that day in 1797 was for many in the audience a symbol of the country's unity and common destiny. In his speech the new president declared, "What other form of government, indeed, can so well deserve our esteem and love?"

Sadly, the harmony was not to last. There remained the question of policy toward France. The French had just seen the United States embracing the British, their archenemy, under the terms of the Jay Treaty. All the earlier attempts by Jefferson as minister to France to establish firm diplomatic

Thomas Jefferson became vice-president without making a speech, issuing a statement, or denouncing his opponents' party. He maintained, in fact, an aloof attitude toward political factionalism. "If I could not go to heaven but with a party," he said, "I would not go there at all."

The U.S.S. *Constitution*, the 44-gun frigate popularly known as "Old Ironsides," fought many of the sea battles that punctuated Franco-American relations in the late 1790s. The American vessel also saw heavy action in the War of 1812, when she effortlessly knocked out such British men-of-war as H.M.S. *Guerrière* (above).

The French navy boasted many fine officers, but its ships were no match for such American frigates as the *United States*, *President*, and *Constitution*, whose clean lines and huge spreads of canvas enabled them to outsail anything afloat. By the end of hostilities, the 54-ship U.S. Navy had captured 93 French vessels.

ties with the French government had now been damaged by mutual distrust. French ships were interfering with United States vessels. French politicians were blasting the United States government as a slave to the British.

In May 1797 in one of his first major decisions as president, Adams appointed a three-man commission to negotiate a treaty with France. It was an effort to calm these scorching political fires and, at the same time, to open up better trading relations between the two countries. The effort was a disaster. In a bitter slap at the United States, three French agents, identified in the commission's reports as X, Y, and Z, agreed to discuss a treaty only if the United States offered a large loan to France and paid a $240,000 bribe to the French foreign minister, Charles Talleyrand. The French threatened war with the United States if the demands were not met. The United States commission refused to deal under these terms. All of this became known in the press as "The XYZ Affair," and it quickly began to shift public opinion against France.

The Adams administration prepared for war. Congress passed numerous measures strengthening the national defense. Existing treaties with France were repealed. Clashes between French and American ships became frequent. A major war, however, never developed, both sides gradually backing off.

But even though the two countries never officially declared war, the hysteria sparked legislation by the Adams administration against foreigners now in the country who might be possible French spies or supporters. The government also moved to silence criticism by pro-French politicians in the Republican party, namely Jefferson and his colleagues.

In 1798 the Federalist-dominated Congress passed the Alien Act, which empowered the president to remove from the country any noncitizens he considered dangerous to the national security. Many of these people, of course, were Republican sympathizers. In addition to the alien law, the Sedition Act provided for fines or even prison sentences for persons convicted of publishing false or malicious

The Bill of Rights—10 constitutional amendments written at the insistence of Jefferson and Madison—guaranteed Americans such rights as freedom of speech and religion. The amendments went into effect in 1791, after 11 states had ratified them, but Massachusetts, Connecticut, and Georgia did not offically approve them until 1939.

statements against the government, Congress, or the president. The Federalists were striking back at their hated tormentors, the Republicans.

This time, however, the Federalists had gone too far. The measures seemed to many in the country a violation of the freedom of speech and freedom of the press guaranteed by the Constitution. What right did the present government have to choke off criticism by the Republican opposition? Did not the Constitution preserve the right of individuals to speak freely against the government and its policies? By strangling their opponents the Federalists were at the same time strangling basic personal liberties.

This was a "Reign of Terror," the Republicans cried, tyranny of huge dimensions. Jefferson was

Charles Talleyrand (1754–1838), foreign minister in France's post-revolutionary government, demanded a $10 million loan and a huge bribe from the U.S. government in return for signing a peace treaty. The payment was refused, and outraged Americans quickly adopted a new patriotic slogan: "Millions for defense, but not one cent for tribute!"

Maximilien Robespierre (1758–1794), one of the French Revolution's most bloodthirsty leaders, operates a guillotine during the "Reign of Terror," in which tens of thousands of opponents of the revolution were beheaded. The Republicans accused the Federalist Adams administration of creating a similar wave of fear in the United States.

astonished. He believed that the federal government had no authority to enact such measures. The government had only those rights specifically given to it by the people. All other powers remained with the states.

Thomas Jefferson was vice-president of the United States, officially part of the incumbent government led by Federalists. At the same time, he was the leader of the party in opposition. It was a peculiar political situation, one riddled with problems. Open defiance of the government of which he was a part would appear almost traitorous and would give the appearance of a man grasping for power. On the other hand, to sit back and say nothing would be to abandon his principles.

Gathering together some of his Republican friends, Jefferson decided to make the case against the Alien and Sedition Acts. He would not do it, however, through a statement officially made as vice-president, but through a protest secretly written by him and delivered by others. The protest was later known as the Kentucky Resolutions. The Jefferson document was presented to the state legislature of Kentucky and was printed throughout the country.

It was a strong plea for the rights of the states. Whenever the federal government takes power not specifically given to it in the Constitution, the document declared, the states have the right to consider the government's laws as illegal and not in force. The Alien and Sedition Acts were such laws. Jefferson did not advocate open rebellion against the government over these laws. He was merely defining a principle through which the central government's powers would be placed in check. The dangers of the government seizing too much power, he believed, were never more obvious than in the recent actions of the Federalists.

Although Jefferson and the Republicans lacked the power and votes to overturn the Federalist laws, the election of 1800 lay ahead. The philosopher of Monticello, the gentleman farmer, the man who despised much of the political environment, was now determined to put his heart and genius into ousting the Federalists from power. Virginia's famous man of letters and learning was also a crafty political organizer. He geared up to take on John Adams. This time it would not be as a reluctant candidate, but as an eager, driven one.

Not wanting to appear a common political huckster, Jefferson maintained a deceptively low profile during the campaign. He contacted newpaper publishers friendly to Republicans to coordinate articles and strategies of attack. He met behind the scenes with various members of the party, soothing personal quarrels and tensions among them. He wrote many letters, some of them unsigned.

Luck favored the Republicans and Jefferson in 1800. A bitter feud between Adams's supporters and those of Hamilton hopelessly divided the Federalists. Thomas Jefferson defeated John Adams in the popular vote. Because of circumstances surrounding the election process, however, Jefferson's victory was still not established. The Republicans had selected Aaron Burr, Hamilton's enemy from New York, to be Jefferson's running mate. When the votes in the electoral college were counted, Jefferson and Burr had tied. Jefferson and his friends assumed, as did most other people in the country, that Jefferson was now elected. Not yet!

Under the system then in place, the electoral voters did not specify for which office, president or vice-president, their ballots were cast. Because of the tie between Jefferson and Burr, the House of Representatives would select the president. For a time, Burr's supporters in the House blocked Jefferson's election. Through an agonizing 35 roll calls the process continued. Angry supporters of Jefferson jammed the paths and entrance ways to the hall of Congress, demanding that the election not be stolen by the thief Burr. One observer described the mob gathered on the hillside as a "thundercloud over the Capitol." Finally, on the 36th ballot, Jefferson gained the necessary votes for election. He was now president. Some people called the Virginian's election a revolution. Others called it a catastrophe. Jefferson was "Mad Tom" to his enemies; an apostle of freedom to his friends.

"Mad Tom in a Rage" was the title of this anti-Jefferson cartoon. The Federalists often showed "Tom" as a liquor-soaked anarchist trying to destroy the government. Here, aided by the devil, he says, "With the assistance of my old friend and a little more brandy, I will bring it [the government] down."

8

The White House

Washington, D.C., March 4, 1801, Inauguration Day. At Conrad & McMunn's Boarding House near Capitol Hill, Thomas Jefferson, president-elect, quietly dresses. Virginia militiamen parade along the streets. The sound of distant artillery blasts echoes faintly. Jefferson's inauguration is the first to be held in Washington. It is to be modest, no grand day of ceremony, no sumptuous banquets, no gala balls. There is not even a coach to carry the new leader of the United States to the Capitol. He will walk. Shortly before 9:00 a.m., surrounded by friends and members of Congress, the plainly dressed Jefferson strides toward the Capitol.

The image was thus established. This was to be a government that stood for all citizens regardless of their social class, a government responsible to all of its people. In the Senate chamber, Jefferson took the oath of office and delivered his inaugural address, calling for Republicans and Federalists alike to put aside political differences and work together for the common good. "We are all Republicans; we are all Federalists," he declared. He called for tolerance, peace, equal justice for all, and for national growth and unity. He called the United States "the world's best hope."

Jefferson's election to the presidency, regarded as a catastrophe by most Federalists, was greeted by Republicans as the dawn of a new golden age. His administration, said one optimistic observer, would guarantee the "propagation of the Rights of Man, the eradication of hierarchy, oppression, superstition, and tyranny all over the world."

Jefferson was inaugurated in the new Capitol building, which later housed the Supreme Court. In 1801, Washington consisted of a few elegant structures on a muddy strip of land between a forest and the Potomac River. Pennsylvania Avenue was a stump-filled dirt road that ran through a swamp to the White House.

Dolly Todd Madison (1768–1849) was a lively and popular young widow when she met and married James Madison, who was 17 years her senior. She became a celebrated Washington hostess during her husband's terms as secretary of state and president.

What kind of president would the tall, lanky Virginian prove to be? That question dominated the thoughts of enemies and friends alike. The president of Yale University, Timothy Dwight, warned that the country was about to be "governed by blockheads." Elderly ladies in Boston, some said, hid their Bibles under mattresses as the Virginian "atheist" took over. But in Philadelphia a group made its way from the State House to the German Reformed Church to hear a reading of the Declaration of Independence. A citizens' committee in Lexington, Kentucky, soon reported to the new president that schoolteachers were asking students to memorize his inaugural address.

Jefferson himself looked upon his new administration as revolutionary, a new experiment in government. "The eyes of suffering humanity are fixed on us with anxiety as their only hope," he wrote.

Sensing that the Federalist party was slipping down a steep hill to destruction, Jefferson was determined to give it a formidable shove in that direction. In extending a hand of peace to some of the moderate Federalists, he hoped to divide them from their more extreme colleagues, those led by Hamilton. In that way, Jefferson felt, the Republican Party would become dominant for years to come.

Jefferson selected his close friend James Madison to be secretary of state. He chose the Swiss-born Albert Gallatin of Pennsylvania to be secretary of the treasury. The extraordinarily able Gallatin was a trusted Jefferson supporter and the only financial expert of note in the Republican ranks. In other cabinet posts and in various appointments, Jefferson picked several men from New England, the Federalist heartland. It was a further effort to broaden the Republican base of support.

Jefferson was now in the new president's home on Pennsylvania Avenue, a great stone edifice, as yet without the porticoes so familiar to Americans today. It was large enough for "two emperors, one pope, and the grand lama in the bargain," a newspaper reporter wrote. Jefferson's small staff hardly filled it. He worked in the library at the southwest corner.

Albert Gallatin (1761–1849), the aristocratic Swiss native named by Jefferson to head the Treasury Department, was known as "the Wizard of Finance." He managed to reduce the national debt from $80 million to $45 million during his 10 years in office.

The White House had no first lady. Jefferson's daughters were in Virginia raising young families. For a time James Madison and his wife, Dolly, stayed with Jefferson. On occasion, the president hosted large dinners. He usually dressed in plain clothes that contrasted sharply with the elegant attire of most Federalists. He did have a French chef and he introduced new, exotic foods to the guests. One of the novelties was ice cream, made from a recipe he discovered in France. He spent much time in the White House landscaping the grounds and installing gadgets, just as he did at Monticello. But the place generally seemed cold and impersonal.

Washington itself consisted mostly of a few new government buildings separated by vast, muddy, unpaved distances. It was hardly Paris, and Jefferson frequently escaped to Monticello, a little over a hundred miles away.

As he launched his new "revolution," Jefferson aimed to steer the government toward fiscal responsibility, reduce the national debt, cut federal spending, and soothe international tensions—to

John Marshall (1755–1835) served as chief justice of the Supreme Court from 1801 to 1835. Although he was a staunch Federalist, his many important decisions—which established fundamental principles for interpreting the Constitution—were remarkably free of political bias.

Napoleon I (1769–1821), became ruler of France in 1799; after gaining control of most of central Europe, he dreamed of establishing an empire in the New World. His disastrous 1802 attempt to conquer Haiti, however, led him to abandon this grandiose scheme, and to sell Louisiana to the United States in 1803.

undo, in other words, much of the effects of previous administrations' policies.

Soon after becoming president, Jefferson confronted a tricky political problem. John Adams, shortly before leaving office, had appointed over 40 Federalists as judges, positions from which they could not be removed and from which they could continue to influence public policy in the Federalist mold. Because the appointments were made at the last minute, the men became known as the "midnight judges." By the time Adams left office, the commissions for the judges had been signed by him but not yet delivered to the men themselves. Outraged by the effort of Adams to pack the judiciary, Jefferson refused to allow Secretary of State

Jefferson's purchase of Louisiana advanced the border of the United States to the Rocky Mountains. About 40,000 Creoles—descendants of French or Spanish immigrants—and their slaves lived on the banks of the lower Mississippi, but less than 1% of the territory was settled when the United States acquired it.

Madison to deliver the appointment papers, as was the normal practice. Led by William Marbury, four of the nominees took the case to the Supreme Court, presided over by Chief Justice John Marshall of Virginia, a Federalist and political foe of Jefferson.

Marshall's decision in *Marbury* vs. *Madison* was a landmark in judicial and political history. The Court ruled that Marbury should not have been denied his appointment. At the same time, however, the Court declared that the law through which Marbury had approached the Supreme Court for assistance was not constitutional. The case estab-

William Clark (1770–1838) was invited by Meriwether Lewis to join him on the quest for a water route to the Pacific Ocean. A journal written by the pair, *History of the Expedition Under the Commands of Captains Lewis and Clark*, became a bestseller in 1814.

lished what is now called "judicial review," the right of the Supreme Court to declare a law of Congress unconstitutional and to abolish it. Jefferson never accepted judicial review as valid and the Court never found another opportunity during his administration to rule on such a case. But later, long after Jefferson had left office, judicial review became an important feature of the United States legislative process. For now, however, Jefferson prevailed. The midnight judges did not take office and judicial review never affected his presidency.

What did affect his administration was a mysterious territory in the west. A land of swamps and uncharted waters, wide plains and dense forests, fertile soil and bands of roving Indians, this area—called Louisiana—seemed to be of possible promise to the United States. The land was at the time largely unsettled, its native serenity disturbed only by traders and trappers. Cutting through it was the Mississippi River, which snaked its way to the port of New Orleans and the Gulf of Mexico.

Jefferson had spoken of the United States as a "chosen country," separated by oceans from the turmoils of the world, having room enough for expansion for a thousand generations. In 1802 that land seemed suddenly threatened. Spain had handed over its Louisiana lands to France, now led by Napoleon Bonaparte, a man ambitious to establish an empire in the region of the Gulf of Mexico and the Caribbean. Jefferson and many others in the United States saw Napoleon's design as a threat to the future of the country.

Resisting a rising chorus of voices calling for war measures against France, Jefferson tried diplomacy. He sent James Monroe to Paris to offer $10 million for the port of New Orleans. Astonishingly, the French asked if the United States wanted the whole region. Napoleon's fortunes had turned sour. He had lost much of his army to yellow fever in the Caribbean and had seen his fleet icebound in Holland. With his visions of an empire in the Americas crumbling, Napoleon decided in 1803 to sign away Louisiana. He hoped to gain in the sale an ally against England at the same time that he was

Meriwether Lewis (1774—1809), co-leader of the expedition that explored the Louisiana Purchase territories, became governor of the territory in 1807. Beset by financial problems arising from his land speculations, and questioned by the government about his use of public funds, Lewis killed himself at the age of 35.

picking up needed cash. The final price was $11,250,000. For only a small amount more than he was willing to pay for New Orleans, Jefferson had acquired over 800,000 square miles of rich agricultural land, most of it between the Mississippi River and the Rocky Mountains. The purchase doubled the size of the United States.

Federalists screamed that the land was useless, that this was all a plot to add new Republican states, that Jefferson had no constitutional authority to purchase the land. The last was a charge Jefferson had difficulty refuting.

The man who had for so long insisted on a narrow view of the powers of the president under the Constitution was now stretching his philosophy to its limits. He did it, he said, from "necessity," and

Lewis and Clark meet with Shoshone Indians in the Rocky Mountain foothills. Thanks to the explorers' interpreter, a Shoshone named Sacajawea ("Bird Woman") who traveled with them, they were able to converse with the various tribes they encountered, all of whom were friendly.

to save the country. The country was behind him. It celebrated one of the most remarkable real estate deals in history.

What was out there in the western wilderness? What would all of this new land mean to the United States? Even before the Lousiana Purchase, Jefferson had planned to send an expedition to the region to chart its geography and to gain knowledge about its plant and animal life and Indians. His own curiosity hungered for answers.

To lead the expedition he chose his close friend and secretary, Meriwether Lewis, a man from Jefferson's own Albemarle County. After spending time learning mapmaking and other scientific skills, Lewis set out for Illinois to recruit and train an exploring party. He carried with him money from Congress and detailed instructions from Jefferson. At Lewis's request, a share of the command was given to his old army friend, Captain William Clark. Jefferson's plan envisaged navigating the Missouri River to its source and attempting to reach the Pacific Ocean. Such a trip had never been made before, not by the French, English, or Spanish, not by trappers or traders.

In May 1804 three well-stocked boats entered the Missouri to begin one of the most legendary journeys in American history. For more than two years the party persevered against incredible hardships—

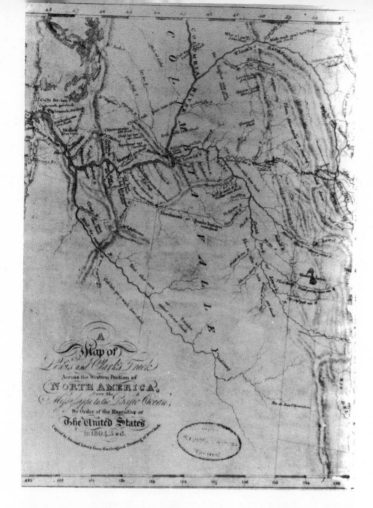

This "Map of Lewis and Clark's Track Across the Western Portion of North America" was published soon after the explorers' return to the east coast. Lewis and Clark's minutely detailed journals and reports are still a valuable source of information on the Far West in the 19th century.

disease, overturned boats, grizzly bears, rattlesnakes, terrible weather, inadequate food supplies, baffling terrain, terrifying rapids, skirmishes with Indians, and, most of all, the unknown. For many months, the explorers had been given up for dead, and Jefferson anguished over his role in sponsoring so dangerous an expedition. But in the face of staggering odds, the expedition finally returned, bringing with it an amazing wealth of information. Early on the day of his arrival in St. Louis, Lewis wrote to Jefferson that they had returned from the Pacific. Jefferson received the news, he said, with "unspeakable joy."

The Lewis and Clark expedition had been a remarkable demonstration of courage, persistence, and skill. It was symbolic, Jefferson thought, of the strength and potential of the new nation.

9
The Second Term

Meriwether Lewis and William Clark, both good Republicans, were pleased to discover on their return that their president and party were enjoying prosperity. By 1806 the Republicans controlled the White House, Congress, and most of the state governments. The 1804 election was one of the most lopsided in American history. Jefferson carried almost every state against Federalist Charles Cotesworth Pinckney. Although he had first vowed to return to Monticello after only a single term, Jefferson now was comfortable in the presidency, still anxious to set straight what he saw as the evils of the first two administrations.

His vice-president for the second term was George Clinton, seven-time governor of New York. It was not Aaron Burr. In one of the most startling occurrences in the life of the young country, first-term vice-president Burr had killed Alexander Hamilton in a duel on the banks of the Hudson River. The two had been bitter enemies for years, but Hamilton's death was truly shocking to Jefferson. Burr fled after the duel and for the next three years engaged in a bizarre plot to establish an independent nation in the west, a conspiracy that was to involve Spain. His scheme later discovered, Burr

Charles C. Pinckney (1746–1825) of South Carolina was an unsuccessful candidate for vice-president in 1800 and for president in 1804 and 1808. He was one of the American delegates who rejected the demand of French Foreign Minister Talleyrand for a bribe in the infamous "XYZ affair" of 1797.

Jefferson was riding high in 1804. Even John Randolph, a congressman noted for his scathing remarks, was enthusiastic. "Never," he said, "was there an administration more brilliant... taxes repealed; the public debt amply provided for...Louisiana acquired; public confidence unbounded." The euphoria, unfortunately, did not last.

George Clinton (1739–1812) became Jefferson's vice-president in 1804. This was the first election held after Amendment XII was passed, making it impossible to question which man had been elected for which office. From this point on, presidents were specifically voted for as presidents, and vice-presidents as vice-presidents.

was arrested on charges of treason but was acquitted for lack of evidence.

Jefferson was outraged at Burr's acquittal. The incident demonstrated, he thought, just how fragile the country was, how vulnerable to plotters and outlaws. The United States was still very much a land of the frontier, a country open to swift change. The president, a man who had consistently argued against a strong central government and against a large military, now feared a lack of stability in the country and perceived a need to protect it.

In his second term, Jefferson wrestled constantly with matters of national defense. In Europe the never-ending struggle between England and France had escalated once again, and Jefferson vowed to remain neutral, to "cultivate the friendship" of both countries. Such a position was becoming more difficult. Both combatants were interfering with United States shipping on the high seas. The British had even begun kidnapping American sailors from waterfront locations and from American merchant ships at sea. In some ways the British navy had become like a band of pirates.

Federalists lambasted Jefferson for allowing such humiliation of Americans. Their protests became wild cries for war after June 1807. In that month the British frigate *Leopard* stopped the American naval ship *Chesapeake* about 10 miles out of Nor-

Aaron Burr and Alexander Hamilton fight a duel in Weehawken, New Jersey, on July 11, 1804. Hamilton, who did not believe in dueling, had accepted Burr's challenge in order to prove his courage, but he deliberately threw away his fire. Burr aimed to kill, and Hamilton, shot in the chest, died 30 hours later.

folk, Virginia. The British commander accused the Americans of harboring four British deserters. When the Americans refused to turn over the men, the *Leopard* opened fire, killing four Americans and injuring many others. "Never since the battle of Lexington have I seen this country in such a state of exasperation," Jefferson wrote. In mass meetings across the country, groups demanded war. After seeing large numbers of people gather at a public demonstration in Baltimore, one United States senator wrote, "There appeared but one opinion—war."

Jefferson chose peace. The country was in no condition to march off to battle as the populace wished. The navy was relatively weak and stood no chance whatsoever of fighting the British effectively. The cost of war to the young nation, now only in its second generation, could be of tragic proportions, Jefferson believed.

The appearance of supply-laden British merchant vessels like these was welcomed by American colonists in the 1700s. By the early 19th century, however, the sight of a ship flying the Union Jack signaled trouble: robbery, the kidnapping of American seamen, and, sometimes, death.

The federal government, in the form of a snapping turtle, prevents a merchant from loading his goods on a British vessel. The 14-month-long "ograbme" ("embargo" spelled backward) was Jefferson's most unpopular act. He authorized its repeal on March 1, 1809, three days before the end of his second term.

But given the mood of the country, Jefferson could not sit idle. He made provisions for strengthening the armed forces. He also decided to boycott all British and French goods. Under terms of the Embargo Act of 1807 Americans could engage in no trade with Britain and France, normally America's chief trading partners.

Unfortunately, the embargo seemed to injure only American shippers; the British and French were less dependent on American trade than Jefferson believed. The policy became something of a national embarrassment. Not only the Federalists, but many other Americans felt that the national honor remained unavenged. They still wanted war.

As his second term drew to a close with war fever searing the nation, Jefferson's position recalled for some the last days of his governorship of Virginia during the Revolution. He was leaving amidst charges that he failed in a wartime situation. For those, however, who saw little benefit to be gained and much to be lost by American participation in a war, Jefferson's strong resistance to the growing hysteria, to the angry, scathing attacks on his character, to the pleas even of some of his friends, seemed an act of political courage. He left the presidency once again looking forward to retirement from public life. Monticello, his haven, awaited.

Tranquility is the old man's milk. I go to enjoy it in a few days, and to exchange the roar and tumult of bulls and bears, for the prattle of my grandchildren.
—THOMAS JEFFERSON
writing in 1797

10

The Sage of Monticello

This time the homecoming will be lasting. This time Jefferson returns to Monticello to stay. Monticello! If ever a home reflects the personality of its owner it is Monticello.

From the outside, the home appears modest in size, its gentle shapes nestling in the wooded setting. Walking through the porticoed entrance, a visitor discovers a wondrous museum—mastodon bones and tusks, Indian relics and artifacts from the Lewis and Clark expedition, antlers of American moose, elk, and deer, a buffalo head. The visitor also sees selections of minerals, crystals, and shells, as well as maps, sculpture, and paintings of religious subjects—even a model of the Great Pyramid. Above the door is a calendar clock invented by Jefferson. It is run by cannonball-like weights that move slowly down the wall indicating the days of the week. A copper gong on the roof sounds the hour.

In his study is a revolving chair and revolving-top table on which sits his polygraph, a duplicating writing device, another of Jefferson's inventions. When Jefferson writes with one pen, another pen automatically moves making exact copies of letters and other papers. On a small platform at the south window is his telescope. Lining the room are shelves

Jefferson spent 35 years building his beloved Monticello, which he never truly finished. "And so I hope it will remain all my life," he once said, "as architecture is my delight, and putting up and pulling down one of my favorite amusements."

When you were old the god of government / Seemed to recede a pace, and you were glad. / You watched the masons through your telescope / Finish your school of freedom. Death itself / Stood thoughtful at your bed.
—KARL SHAPIRO modern American poet, in his poem *Jefferson*

Monticello's entrance hall still contains several original Jefferson inventions. Among these are the clock, the folding ladder that was used to reach the clock's winding mechanism, and the double, glass-and-mahogany doors, which contain a hidden device that opens both doors when one is pulled.

Jefferson's polygraph—the forerunner of today's high-speed copiers—was inspired by a model he had seen in France. The original was bulky and difficult to operate, but the concept intrigued Jefferson, who tinkered patiently until he had devised an efficient portable version. He was so pleased with it that he had replicas made for friends.

holding hundreds of books, all carefully arranged by subject.

In the parlor are over 40 paintings. Many of the furnishings are purchases made in Paris—large mirrors, a marble clock, mahogany armchairs.

The dining room features a mechanical dumbwaiter devised by Jefferson by which it is possible to bring wine directly up from the cellar. A serving door pivots in one of the passageways leading to the kitchen. Servants from the kitchen place food on the shelves of the door; servants in the dining room bring the food to the table.

The bedrooms have skylights, double-sealed entrance doors to ward off noise, and windows of double glass to seal out extreme cold. Passageways run from the main part of the house to the wine room, rum cellar, beer room, smokeroom, dairy, servants' quarters, icehouse, laundry room, stables, and kitchen, all built into the hillside. Outside are the nailery, the blacksmithing building, and the weavers' room. Jefferson supervises in great detail the work that goes on in all of these places. He constantly seeks new innovations for them.

Outside also are the flower garden, the grove,

and the vegetable garden, all designed by Jefferson, all filled with an astonishing variety of plants, shrubs, and trees, all the subject of careful scrutiny and exacting notetaking by the head of the household.

An oasis for learning, experimenting, observing, teaching, building, and tinkering, Monticello is a testament to Jefferson's fertile brain.

Jefferson was just about to turn 66 when he left the presidency. Although never again venturing far from Monticello in his remaining years, he continued to follow politics. In dismay he watched the tentacles of the War of 1812 engulf his successor in the presidency, James Madison. He learned with much sadness of the destruction of many of Washington's public buildings by the invading British. Especially indignant over the senseless destruction of the Congressional library, he immediately offered for sale to Congress 13,000 volumes from his own splendid collection of books, gathered from bookstores and private individuals all around the world. Jefferson's collection later became the nucleus for a restored Library of Congress.

Jefferson's last great project, one that now seems particularly fitting and appropriate, sprang from his lifelong commitment to education. It had been over 25 years since he outlined a plan for public education in Virginia. He returned to the subject again and again, pushing for elementary schools in every county, district high schools accessible to all families, free advanced schooling for students of exceptional abilities whose parents were poor, and a state university.

As early as 1800 Jefferson had called for a "Uni-

> *Every child in a democracy who is to learn to develop himself into a true citizen of his own nation, should not only study the life of Jefferson, but his philosophy, which set the things of the mind and of the heart above material things and made material things serve the ends which the mind and heart conceived.*
> —ELEANOR ROOSEVELT

Jefferson's bedroom, whose walls were painted with classical Roman-style decorations, contained a curtained sleeping alcove in which laced-cord bedsprings were suspended from iron hooks in the wall. This made it possible to use the bedroom as a study or sitting room during the day.

Monticello, as revealed by this bird's-eye view, is laid out in the shape of a capital letter E. Underground passages connect the main building (center) with the wings containing the slave quarters (on the lower bar of the E) and the storerooms and workshops (upper bar).

Education engrafts a new man on the native stock, and improves what in his nature was vicious and perverse into qualities of virtue and social worth.

—THOMAS JEFFERSON
quoted from the *Report of the Commissioners for the University of Virginia* of 1818

versity on a plan so broad and liberal and *modern*, as to be worth patronizing with the public support." He made proposals for the university's curriculum, the faculty to be recruited, the financing, and even the architecture of its buildings. With the help of friends and benefactors, Jefferson purchased an old academy in nearby Charlottesville, the site on which the new university would be built. In 1816 the state legislature incorporated the school as Central College, and within three years the University of Virginia was born. Thomas Jefferson was named the school's rector.

Through all of the construction of the university, Jefferson was there, designing, planning, organizing. He brought skilled craftsmen to carve the stone; he found gifted teachers. Not surprisingly, Jefferson was especially absorbed in the building of the library. Its center structure would be a rotunda, its ceiling sky blue and "spangled with gilt stars in their position and magnitude copied exactly from any selected hemisphere of our latitude." The library rotunda was thus a planetarium.

Several of Jefferson's friends remembered his grandchildren following him around the grounds and gardens of Monticello in his last years. The sight of Jefferson directing children's footraces on the Monticello lawn was a common sight. Another was Jefferson talking to the children about their education, about the marvelous riches that lay ahead for each one of them in their own lives if only they looked and studied and reasoned and explored. Education, learning, the need to understand, the freedom to discover, the right to achieve as much as one's talents and industry allow—for these aspirations Jefferson firmly stood. He once wrote, "I have sworn upon the altar of God, eternal hostility against every form of tyranny over the mind of man." He devoted his life's work to this principle. Late in his life Jefferson asked that on his grave only three accomplishments be listed: that he wrote the Declaration of Independence, that he authored the Virginia statute for religious freedom, and that he was the father of the University of Virginia.

In a key battle of the War of 1812, Colonel James Miller leads his regiment against British artillery at Niagara Falls, New York. A month later, in August 1814, the British invasion of Baltimore (where Francis Scott Key wrote "The Star-Spangled Banner") was repelled; the costly war ended the following December.

Jefferson directed that his tombstone be made of "coarse stone," to prevent its theft "for the value of the materials." Within a half-century of his death, however, souvenir-hunters had chipped away most of the original granite obelisk. Congress replaced it with the larger monument that now guards his grave.

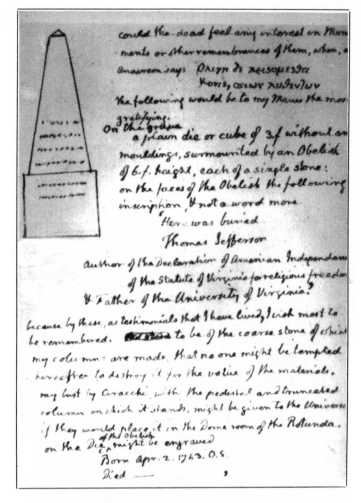

Ten days before he died, Jefferson wrote his last letter. He had been invited to attend ceremonies in Washington, D.C. commemorating the 50th anniversary of the Declaration of Independence. As he thought back to those days in Philadelphia a half-century earlier, he still found faith in the goals of personal freedom and liberty so eloquently phrased in the Declaration. In his letter he wrote, "All eyes are opened, or opening to the rights of man . . . the mass of mankind has not been born with saddles on their backs, nor a favored few booted and spurred, ready to ride them legitimately, by the grace of God. These are grounds of hope for others. For ourselves, let the annual return of this day, forever refresh our recollections of those rights, and an undiminished devotion to them."

On July 3, 1826, Jefferson awoke at about 7:00 p.m. and asked his doctor, "Is it the Fourth?" The next day, the 50th anniversary of the Declaration of Independence, Jefferson died at age 83. Remarkably, on the very same day in Quincy, Massachusetts, John Adams, Jefferson's old friend and fellow revolutionary, also died. At Adams's bedside a friend heard him remark, "Thomas Jefferson still survives."

In so many ways, he does indeed.

But though an old man, I am but a young gardener.
—THOMAS JEFFERSON

At the age of 78, Jefferson posed for artist Thomas Sully (1783–1872), who also painted *Washington Crossing the Delaware*. The nation's third president has inspired millions of words, none more apt, perhaps, than those of a successor. "The principles of Jefferson," said President Abraham Lincoln (1809–1865), "are the axioms of a free society."

Further Reading

Chinard, Gilbert. *Thomas Jefferson: The Apostle of Americanism.* Ann Arbor, Michigan: The University of Michigan Press, 1962.

Graff, Henry F. *Thomas Jefferson.* Morristown, New Jersey: Silver Burdett Company, 1968.

Malone, Dumas. *Jefferson the Virginian.* Boston: Little, Brown and Company, 1948.

———. *Jefferson and the Rights of Man.* Boston: Little, Brown and Company, 1951.

———. *Jefferson and the Ordeal of Liberty.* Boston: Little, Brown and Company, 1962.

———. *Jefferson the President, First Term, 1801–1805.* Boston: Little, Brown and Company, 1970.

———. *Jefferson the President, Second Term, 1805–1809.* Boston: Little, Brown and Company, 1974.

———. *The Sage of Monticello.* Boston: Little, Brown and Company, 1977.

Peterson, Merrill D. *Thomas Jefferson and the New Nation.* New York: Oxford University Press, 1970.

———, ed. *The Portable Thomas Jefferson.* New York: Penguin Books, 1984.

Chronology

April 13, 1743	Born Thomas Jefferson at Shadwell Plantation, Virginia
1762	Begins law apprenticeship
1765	British Parliament passes Stamp Act, a tax on documents, thus provoking widespread hostility among American colonists
Dec. 1768	Jefferson elected to Virginia's House of Burgesses
1769	House of Burgesses rules that British Parliament cannot tax Virginia's citizens
March 5, 1770	British soldiers fire on rioting Boston civilians, killing three, in what disaffected colonists call the "Boston Massacre"
Jan. 1, 1772	Jefferson marries Martha Wayles Skelton
Dec. 1773	Boston Tea Party
1774	Jefferson writes *A Summary View of the Rights of British America*
April 19, 1775	Revolutionaries defeat British at Battle of Lexington
June 1775	Writes *Declaration of the Cause and Necessity for Taking up Arms*
June 1776	Jefferson writes *Declaration of Independence*
July 4, 1776	Twelve out of thirteen colonies approve declaration
1776–79	Jefferson serves in Virginia's assembly
June 1779	Appointed governor of Virginia by state legislature
Jan. 1781	Benedict Arnold, an American loyal to Britain, leads British capture of Richmond, Virginia
Sept. 6, 1782	Martha Jefferson dies
Feb. 3, 1783	Peace treaty with Britain concluded in Paris
May 1784	Jefferson appointed by Congress to three-man commission negotiating commerce with European countries
1785–89	Serves as minister to France
1790	Jefferson becomes first U.S. secretary of state
1796	Elected vice-president
1798	Writes Kentucky Resolutions
March 4, 1801	Becomes third president of the United States
April 30, 1803	United States purchases province of Louisiana from France for $12 million, thus doubling national territory
1804	Jefferson elected to second term as president
1809–15	United States clashes with Britain in conflict later known as the War of 1812
1809	Jefferson retires to Monticello, his family home in Virginia, as a private citizen
1816–19	Helps establish University of Virginia and is named rector
July 4, 1826	Dies, aged 83, at Monticello, of natural causes

Roger Bruns is Director of Publications of the National Historical Publications and Records Commission in Washington, D.C. His most recent book is *Knights of the Road: A Hobo History*, published by Methuen, Inc., in 1980. He has just completed a biography of the social reformer Ben Reitman.

Arthur M. Schlesinger, jr., taught history at Harvard for many years and is currently Albert Schweitzer Professor of the Humanities at City University of New York. He is the author of numerous highly praised works in American history and has twice been awarded the Pulitzer Prize. He served in the White House as special assistant to presidents Kennedy and Johnson.